"JIMMY DUNNE SAYS"

47 SHORT STORIES THAT ARE SURE TO
MAKE YOU LAUGH, CRY – AND THINK

"JIMMY DUNNE SAYS"
AMERICA'S NEW, POSITIVE
& INSPIRING VOICE

JIMMY DUNNE

SAVIO
REPVBLIC

A SAVIO REPUBLIC BOOK
An Imprint of Post Hill Press
ISBN: 979-8-88845-360-5
ISBN (eBook): 979-8-88845-361-2

Jimmy Dunne Says:
47 Short Stories That Are Sure to Make You Laugh, Cry—and Think
© 2024 by Jimmy Dunne
All Rights Reserved

Cover Design by Conroy Accord

posthillpress.com
New York • Nashville
Published in the United States of America

1 2 3 4 5 6 7 8 9 10

Dedication

I thought a lot about this, and the only honest answer is...
You.
That's who this is for. That's who this is about.
If a few of these stories hit a nerve, touch you, take you back
to a moment in your life, or just rub your neck a little bit
before you go out there swinging in the next round...
Cheers to *you.*

Jimmy Dunne

TABLE OF CONTENTS

INTRODUCTION

Abbout me.

I've been blessed to have a career doing what I absolutely love and with a lot of lucky breaks along the way. In my personal life, my wife, Catherine, and two daughters, Kaitlyn and Alexis, my grandson, and my son-in-law make me the luckiest guy in the world.

Throw in the soup growing up in a parish and a Chicago suburban town with the richest soil and the heartiest roots in the world.

All that in a home with two spectacular, giving parents and six brothers and sisters whom I can't love and respect more.

I give thanks every single day for the lake full of inspiring friends from my growing up days, college days in Kentucky, and my adult journey in California.

I've been blessed with an abundance of selfless teachers and mentors—along with the privilege of collaborating with many of the country's most creative talents and business minds across eclectic disciplines.

These are short stories I've written since my kids were little squirts.

They've found their way into our town paper, papers around the country, magazines, and various mediums along the way.

✳ ✳ ✳

Here's why I want to share them with you.

It's kind of like a nearby fire.

First, you see it in the sky.

Then you start to feel it in the air when you breathe. There's a thickness. It's *dirty*. You just *know* it's not healthy for you.

And you wake up in the morning, and *there* it is—it has covered your car. The soot. It's permeated *everything*.

That's where we're at.

In America. In the world.

The anger. The divisiveness. The hurt. The pain.

It's seeping in and around *everything*.

Truth is, for most of the issues on the skillet, there's not a lot any of us can do about it.

But we've got to make sure this soot doesn't get in our lungs—and our kids' lungs.

And I think I know *how*.

* * *

Einstein told a story about when he was a seven-year-old kid. How his dad gave him a compass. And how he couldn't get over how the needle *always* pointed north. How something *invisible*, that he couldn't see, made it *do* that.

He said he'd been chasing the *same* thing his whole life. A glimpse of that *deeply* hidden thing.

Finding the *wonder*.

And I believe it's right in our *own* backyards.

In our lives. In our families. In our friends. In our towns.

The absolute *wonder* of life.

Those unexpected moments—there for us to *behold*.

May these stories remind you of moments, of people, of places that take you back, that paint a picture of how lucky you and I are.

Of what an amazing treasure chest life is.

And may you share the *wonder* in you with the world.

DOWNSIZING

My wife, Catherine, and I recently moved.
I realized I had something I *never* knew I had.

Thirty-four years ago, I carried my wife in my arms over the threshold into our home. *Thirty-four* years ago. From newlywed days to witnessing our babies go from little girls to young adults.

So many great memories in *every inch* of every room of our home.

I didn't think I was ready to "downsize."

What an awful word.

I *liked* walking through our girls' bedrooms and still seeing their stuff on the walls and on the shelves. I *liked* our backyard. I *liked* imagining our kids coming down the steps every Christmas morning.

We put it on the market, it sold in a week, and suddenly agreements thicker than my leg were instructing me to clear everything I ever had and knew—*out*.

＊ ＊ ＊

Every night, I found myself saying goodbye to our backyard. To our garden of roses that Catherine would till and trim.

To the sidewalk, where the girls drove their Barbie cars and learned to ride their bikes. To our front lawn, where we hosted tons of talent shows with all the kids on the block. To the red swing on the front porch.

We found a condo in town and started lining up our ducks of what we were keeping—and what we were tossing.

We vowed if we were going to do this, we weren't putting *anything* in storage.

I literally threw out half my stuff. *Half.* Half of the furniture. Half of my clothes, books.

＊ ＊ ＊

And the big one. *Half* of the boxes in the attic.

The attic was more than an attic. It held our stories. Everything in every box, every framed picture, was a *story*.

We brought down everything of the girls' from the attic—and we split the living room in half.

We invited the girls over, handed 'em a cocktail, and said, "There's good news and bad news.

"We've saved all this stuff—your outfits, drawings, dolls, skates—for *you*.

It's now *yours*.

"The *bad* news: whatever's not gone by Friday at ten in the morning, it's getting chucked in that giant green dumpster in front of the house."

The girls thought we were Mr. and Mrs. Satan.

But they went through it, and by Friday, most went right in the dumpster.

I filled the *entire* dining room with boxes of all my old stuff. Grade-school stories and pictures, report cards, birthday cards, trophies, you name it. Boxes of old plaques and diplomas and just stuff and stuff and stuff like that.

How could I throw *any* of this out? It was like throwing *me* in the dumpster!

✳ ✳ ✳

But this little jerk on my shoulder kept asking, *what are your kids going to do with all this—one week after you're six feet under? They're gonna chuck it all out!*

Here's the crazy thing. The more I threw stuff in that dumpster, the easier it got. And I started to kind of *like* throwing it up and over in that thing.

I started to feel lighter. *Better.*

And we moved into a half-the-size condo—and the *oddest* thing happened.

It became our *home.*

A picture here and there on the wall, Catherine's favorite pieces of furniture, all her knickknacks in the bathroom. We blinked, and it felt just like *us*.

And then I found that thing I *never* knew I had.

Enough.

I had enough.

The wild thing was that having less *actually* opened the door to so much *more.*

More in my personal life. More in my career. More in *everything.*

All I have to do is look in the eyes of my two girls—and they take me back, every time, to the most beautiful, colorful, emotional scrapbook I could ever *dream* of having.

All I have to do is hold my wife's hand, and it hypnotizes me back to kissing her for the first time, falling in love with everything she did, seeing her in that hospital room holding our first baby for the first time.

It sure seems there is so much more to see, and feel, and be if I have the courage—if I have the will to shape a life that's just...

Enough.

GRAMMIE AND GRAMPIE RULES

My daughter Kaitlyn, her hubby Jimmy, and new baby Whit live *right* across the street from us in town.

We couldn't love it *more*.

Our daughter gave my wife, Catherine, and me a very detailed list called "How to Babysit Whit."

Some real *gems.*

Like, "Rock Whit to sleep in a chair or walk around the room." How did she *think* we were going to rock him to sleep? While we're taking a shower with him?

Another on her list: "He likes to smile before he falls to sleep." Where I grew up, that's called "gas."

Or, "If he stops sucking his bottle, take the bottle out of his mouth and reinsert."

Thanks *so* much. We were thinking we were supposed to shove the bottle in his *ear.*

But my fave is, "If he tries to eat his hands, he's hungry."

That is *so* helpful to know. Maybe the title of a new bestselling parenting book.

* * *

Here's what I'm kind of *missing.* Help me with this.

Memo to Kaitlyn: You *lived* in your mother's belly.

She raised you and your sister.

Hmmm.

Maybe Kaitlyn thinks we can't *remember* how to do *anything* anymore. Maybe *that's* it. Half the time, we *do* call the babe "Louis," our dog. Probably doesn't help.

Life is confusing.

* * *

I was sharing Grammie and Grampie notes with Becky and Jai in town. They don't make 'em better.

They told me about the marching orders *they* got from their daughter, Cami.

I just adore Cami. Cami's got the cutest little boy.

Cami did the *same* thing. Sat her mom and pop down on her living room sofa for a little "Parenting 101."

Jai and Becky got strict marching orders that there would be absolutely *no* drinking while babysitting the precious one. (They *barely* drink.) Jai and Becky just smiled and nodded. "Yes, ma'am."

Now to make sure Grammie and Grampie were following orders, Cami pointed to cameras she installed in her place to *make sure* they were following the rules.

Well, it didn't really play out that way.

Becky and Jai quickly become *experts* at holding the little guy while walking with their wine on their hips "out of the camera's eye." Thank God Cami hasn't caught on.

Whoops. Maybe I shouldn't have put this story in a book.

✳ ✳ ✳

Here's what I know for *sure*. It doesn't get better than *this*.

Babysitting. Best job in the world.

I've gotta run. The baby's crying in Catherine's arms.

Maybe Catherine can't get that bottle in the babe's ear.

GARDENING

It's a spectacular Sunday morning.

I bicycled by a dad gardening in the front lawn of his home. He had a good sweat going on—digging a hole for a little bush.

From the look of his snappy home, he wasn't out there to save a few bucks on a gardening bill.

My guess is he was tapping into something that goes back a couple thousand generations in all of us.

He's tapping into a connection, a need, a gravity to be one with our home. This place we're so privileged to be a guest.

Our extraordinarily amazing, colorful, delicate, evolving earth.

And in planting that bush, in *some* way, we're holding in our hands where we came from.

We're seeding something with the excitement of imagining what it will *become.*

* * *

We're all hurting right now—to varying degrees.

Because of the divisiveness of politics and all it breeds. The looming threats of war, the ever-present nuclear card dangling out there, all things the environment, inflation, Ukraine, AI, Israel-Gaza, just stuff. Just angry, unsettling stuff.

All this stuff ratchets up our worries about what we're handing over to the next generation—and to their children.

We may not feel it, but it's *there* under the surface of it all.

It's *there* at the stop signs when folks are waiting for their turn to go. It's *there* in curt phone conversations we have with people on the other end of a call across the world. In comments on Facebook and blogs.

It's seeping into the roots.

There's a wonderful Ukrainian toast they make at large family events.

They clink their glasses, look each other in the eyes, and say something that translates to, "Know who you are."

What a beautiful thought.

To know who you are.

From the moment of waking into the world in a loving mother's arms, we spend a lifetime trying to uncover the answer to this ultimate puzzle and mystery of life.

Maybe just touching the earth is a good place for us to start.

To show our deference to our home. To remind us to find humility, a thankfulness for who and where we are.

To touch, and feel, and smell, and hear, and witness nature.

Maybe it's making a special weekend morning with our kids or grandkids to stick some bulbs in the soil with our hands.

Maybe it's taking a walk at dusk with our dog—listening to what the swaying trees in town that blanket us may be trying to whisper.

Maybe it's putting our feet in the gentle, lapping water where the warm sand meets the cool hello of the ocean.

Maybe it's a morning picnic at the park with our families where the blue jays, hummingbirds, parakeets, and song sparrows are the loveliest choir in a stunning song.

Or maybe it's biting into an apple, or cherry, or orange—tasting it as we haven't tasted it in a while. And wondering where it was born and where it grew to be as beautiful as it is.

Maybe it's about tonight after we go around our home and turn off all the lights. Stepping out in our backyard all by ourselves.

Looking *up*.

And thinking about how what we see and feel will *never* be exactly this way again.

While we stand so firmly on that rich soil under our feet. That anchors us. That settles us.

That heartens us.

FIRST DATES

Some lanky high school freshman kid with a sea of pimples on his too-red face with that determined look of "One day I'm going to look like John Cusack" knocked on our front door to pick up my daughter Kaitlyn for her first real high school "date."

I waved to his my-age dad, sitting in his car waiting to take them to the freshman dance.

As I shook the kid's hand and looked into his eyes, I spotted that first-date terror festering underneath his goofy, "it's no big deal" grin.

We shook hands longer than he was comfortable with, and I gave him that look of, "I have *no* problem going back to prison again."

And, out of nowhere, it was like that kid and I heard the theme from *Gone with the Wind*—as we turned around to stare at my absolutely stunning daughter waltzing down the staircase.

As she smiled, heading toward that petrified kid—the memory of my first date danced in my head…

* * *

It was my freshman year of high school. Kathy Delaney. God, I was in love with Kathy Delaney. Stunning. Long black hair. A great rack for a freshman.

And beautiful teeth under that wire scaffolding in her mouth.

It was the freshman class homecoming dance. The first real "date" in my life.

Asking Kathy Delaney out was no walk in the park. It was an autumn Monday night, less than two weeks before our high school's homecoming dance.

If I didn't ask her that night, I knew she'd get snatched up by some other freshman clown.

* * *

I swear to God, I came home after school, went upstairs, and spent the next two and a half hours pacing in front of our second-floor hallway yellow rotary phone.

Thinking about *every* possible scenario of how she was going to reject me on that call.

Our freshman "pom pom" cheerleaders. A solar system out of my league.

I *knew* she'd say no. That was a for-sure. I figured it was like original sin; I *deserved* to get no for an answer.

I *had* to call her up, take it like a man, and be done with it.

Come hell or high water, I *was* calling that girl that night.

I didn't care that she was better than me in every way a human being could be better than you. She was Aphrodite. I was Spam.

The clock was ticking.

It was almost six and about time for our brisket of beef family dinner. We had brisket of beef *every* night. Except Fridays, of course. That was Catholic fish sticks night.

I looked at the clock in the bathroom and decided I was pulling the trigger. *I'm walking to that phone, and I'm dialing that number.*

And that's *exactly* what I did.

Then the most horrible thing happened. Kathy answered the phone. It was all happening too fast; it was surreal.

I said, "Kathy?"

She said, "Yes." And then the impossible happened.

My mother, out of absolutely nowhere, came roaring up the staircase with her new Hoover carpet cleaner. It sounded like a helicopter rising up the stairs.

I screamed into the phone, "It's Jimmy Dunne."

"Who?"

"Jimmy Dunne."

"What?"

"Do you want to go to the homecoming dance with me?"

"Who?"

"Jimmy Dunne. You know, from school. Next to your locker."

"Okay."

I couldn't tell for sure what she said with the 747 landing in my other ear.

"Did you say, 'Okay,' or, 'No way'?"

"I said, 'Okay.'"

I never thought that she might say *that*. I didn't elaborate on how much fun I thought we'd have, or where we could go to dinner, or who else I heard was going.

I just hung up.

I didn't even confirm I heard her. I just hung up the damn phone because I didn't know what to say after she said, "Okay."

To punish myself, I walked down those stairs and slugged down four times my normal allotment of fatty brisket of beef.

Here's what our dinner table looked like. I'm sure on this night, we just finished some fine brisket of beef with our two sweet grandmas. I'm not sure why my brother is pointing a gun at the birthday girl while she's blowing out her cake. I'd chalk it up to anger management issues. And I don't know what's wrong with my older sister on the right. Maybe she was still gagging on some of her meat.

* * *

Cut to the next morning.

I got on my school bus, got dumped off at school, and walked up to my locker. With her name being Delaney and mine being Dunne, her locker was *literally* right next to mine.

She was standing there taking her books out and smiling at me like I was her knight or something.

I didn't know what to say to her.

What was I gonna say? "Hey, me and you at the dance in a week and a half!" with an idiot look that says, "I can't *wait* to make out with you"? So I decided to do the *next* best thing.

I pretended she wasn't there. I didn't say *anything*.

She was all confused. In the moment, I could live with that.

Since that was my approach the first day, I figured I'd be consistent. I did that *every day*.

So I never talked to her. Never even looked over at her. She must have thought I was Norman Bates.

A week and a half of locker torture went by, and it was suddenly Friday, the night of the homecoming dance. Like every morning, I walked up to our lockers.

But this morning, she was standing there crying her eyes out.

I said, "What's the matter, Kathy? Did some girl hit you?"

Bawling, she said, "No. The most *horrible* thing happened. Somebody called me two weeks ago, and he said he was you, and he asked me to the dance."

I didn't know what to say.

I said, "That *was* me." She gave me a look like, "Oh, my God. I'm going to a dance with Barney."

Being the sensitive guy I am, I said the only thing that seemed appropriate at that moment.

"So, are we going?"

"Yes, we're *going*," she half-yelled/half-cried at me.

* * *

So, dressed in my one-and-only flame-retardant too-bright-blue suit and tie, holding a boutonniere for Kathy that my mother picked up at Fay Flowers in town, I anxiously sat in the back of my father's yellow Ford Thunderbird—as we crisscrossed through our town's tree-lined suburban streets to Kathy's house.

Everything went smoothly until picture-taking time in Kathy's kitchen.

With her parents clicking and flashing away and her younger brother Chuck snickering nearby, I was posing next to Kathy when I heard this moaning behind me—coming from the kitchen pantry.

It didn't particularly faze me. In our house of seven kids and God only knows what "animals of the month," you deal with it.

But to Kathy, the moaning was like having a zit the size of a cicada on her nose. She snapped around, waving her boutonniere in her hand—yelling at the closet door.

"Get out. Just *get* out. He *knows* you're in there."

I didn't know what she was talking about.

With a meek smile, her very, very short grandma sheepishly squirmed out—and introduced herself to me like it made *perfect* sense she was hiding in the kitchen pantry.

* * *

Off to the dance we went. The dance was a piece of cake.

You just walked around the school gym dance floor in a big circle like it was a roller rink with all the other freshman lemmings. Up on the stage was a jazz combo of bellied, middle-aged, part-time musicians in too-tight gray-blue tuxes playing winners like "Tie a Yellow Ribbon 'Round the Ole Oak Tree."

* * *

My dad picked Kathy and me up from the dance and dropped us at the next stage of our journey.

The Flame; it's an "adult" restaurant in the next town over.

When I say "adult" restaurant, I mean that it was a dark—*really* dark—restaurant where they served steaks with vegetables on the side.

Not the usual nineteen cent White Castle hamburgers fare my refined palate was accustomed to.

As we entered the swanky place, an elevator version of "Sunny" seeped quietly over the speakers tucked behind the plants.

This is where things started to get ugly.

See, I've got this little problem that I didn't foresee when I chose The Flame.

I'm night-blind.

I mean, I'm *really* night-blind.

When I walk in a dark place, it takes me a good hour before I can see my own hands.

I may have been sitting across from her in that restaurant, but she could have been a goat in that chair—and I wouldn't have known the difference.

Not helping the situation was our waiter. A college-aged guy with a thick Argentine accent and long, greasy, curly brown hair who thought he was Ilie Năstase.

He came up to our table and made it perfectly clear to Kathy that his hog was longer and thicker than my leg.

Kathy and I settled into some nice "adult" conversation. I was feeling pretty good about how things were going, other than I was looking across the table into the abyss.

Here's what Kathy looked like to me sitting across the table.

While I was yapping—I just imagined her in her lovely off-white dress, large freshman breasts, and semi-high-heeled shoes with her toes sticking out the front.

I ordered a New York steak. There's no way I could see the menu; I just figured it *had* to be on there in a classy joint like this.

I have to back up for a second.

Coming from a family of seven kids, you ate what was on your plate. In my family, you didn't leave the table until you were a member of the "Clean Plate Club."

To this day, I still think there actually *is* a "Clean Plate Club," and I, unfortunately, have earned "lifelong member" status.

In our house growing up, if you had meat on your plate, you *weren't* getting up.

Fat/no fat, gristle/no gristle—it was going down the hatch.

My brother Terry and I would sit there a half hour after everybody else left the table gnawing on some nasty piece of rubber blubber, imagining we were downing live seventeen-year locusts.

So, when our dinners came, I cut my New York steak with my steak knife—and stuck a big honking piece of it in my mouth.

Whoops.

At least, that's what I *thought* it was when I cut it. It was a glob of fat the size of a ping-pong ball. While I looked at Kathy with a smile on my face, in my heart, I was chewing on an eye.

I had a *plan*.

I nonchalantly put my napkin to my face like I was patting my cheeks and spit the big hunk of blubber in my napkin. As we chatted away, I opened the napkin under our table and dumped the grizzly evidence on the carpet.

Problem solved.

The plan would have worked like a charm, but it landed on her exposed toes. Kathy pulled back from her chair. I asked her what was wrong.

She said something the size of a rat just ran over her right foot.

Next thing you know that Ilie Nastase wannabe had his greasy, mop-top head under our table looking for animals and probably up her dress.

He took his smug head out, flung the greasy hair out of his eyes, and dumped the ball of chewed fat on my plate.

Looking straight at me, he smirked with his Argentine accent, "*There's* your rat."

Just to punish myself, I gobbled down every piece of grizzle on my plate.

We walked out of the restaurant, and there was my smiling Irish dad waiting for us in his Ford Thunderbird.

✳ ✳ ✳

Even though my dad kept yacking it up all the way to Kathy's house, I didn't hear a word. All I was thinking about was her front door.

Her front door. The final frontier.

I was going to walk her to that door, and I was going to kiss her. It was going to be like no other joy I had experienced in my life.

In just a few moments, my lips would be touching hers, and my body would be pressed against her amazing chest...

What more in life could a freshman *possibly* want?

And then, in the middle of that dream, my dad's voice would sneak in. Like a pitchfork in the back of my neck in a bad slasher movie, I'd imagine my dad stretching his head out the driver's seat window, seeing if his kid was scoring at her front door.

When folks talk about the feeling of being ready to parachute out of a plane for the first time, with absolutely no clue of if or where they're landing—*that's* how I felt.

That's what I was dealing with in that back seat of that Thunderbird only blocks from her house—with Kathy, smelling like a fresh bouquet of lilacs, smiling only inches away.

As my dad pulled up to the curb in front of her house, he said, "I'm in no hurry. Take your time." That was short for, "I'm going to be laughing my ass off watching you try to make out with this girl."

We walked, hand in hand, from the sidewalk toward her front door. I felt like the Cowardly Lion heading down the daunting hallway with Dorothy.

The front porch ahead of me looked like a lit-up stage, guaranteed to give my dad a good belly laugh in the car.

Then, a *miracle* happened.

She took my hand and made a right turn. Around the house to her side door. My confidence shot through the roof; she clearly wanted some action.

As we walked along the side of her house in the pitch dark, she literally had to pull my hand like I was a blind person. I couldn't see a foot in front of me.

I kind of tripped up the side stair, and suddenly, there I was, standing there, holding her hand—looking right at her. The moment of truth.

Except I wasn't looking at her; I may have well been looking in a black cave. I knew her face was there because she was holding both my hands. With every passing second, my hands were turning into water faucets.

Rather than just grab her and lay one on her, I stood there babbling just to stall. But I knew the door of the plane was open—and it was time to jump.

I said something absolutely poetic and romantic like, "Well, see ya later, alligator," and leaned in to kiss her lips.

Unfortunately, I missed her lips.

I was kissing something, but it wasn't her lips. It dawned on me I was gnawing on her right ear. Not being an expert on what lips taste or feel like, in that moment of truth, I thought maybe it *was* her lips. Rather than adjust, I just kind of made out with her right ear.

And then I just left. No goodbye. No "I had a nice time." I just left.

I don't know what was worse. Falling on my face after I tripped over the garbage can on the side of her house—or dealing with my dad's shit-eating grin at the car asking me how it *went* with a thumbs up or thumbs down.

Kindly, my dad didn't say a word in the car. We just drove home in the silence.

And there I sat alone in that back seat, letting my mind drift.

Seven or eight blocks later, I forgot about my humiliation, and noticed her lilac scent on my clothes—and reminisced about that spectacular moment of her wanting to lead me to her back door.

✳ ✳ ✳

That's a long story to the five-second middle-age flashback that danced through my head as I watched my stunning daughter Kaitlyn and that lanky kid head out the front door to their dance.

A piece of my childhood ended as he awkwardly opened the door to the back seat of his dad's car on our curb.

And as they drove away, that kid looked back at me through the car's back window.

I politely waved as I thought to myself, *Good luck, schmuck.*

PS: I changed my freshman date's last name. The last thing I'd want is for that girl to have to re-live her first high school date with me.

BUGS IN FRUIT

We all know the saying, "Bugs in fruit."
Comes from the tiny percentage of bug parts the FDA allows for in fruit.

Because bugs *are* on fruit. That's never, ever going to change.

But here's the trick, as we all know.

When we get home, we put the fruit under our faucets—and wash 'em off. Right down the drain they go.

Bye-bye.

Did we get it all? Nope. But good enough. Who cares.

* * *

Bugs in fruit are a lot like jerks.

There are jerks in every town, on every block, in every organization, in every country club, in every business, in every school, church, synagogue—you name it.

There are *always* going to be jerks laying on their horns at stoplights. Jerks walking dogs and not cleaning up. Selfish jerks.

Whether they say it out loud or not, each sentence starts with, "Let me tell you what's good for *me*."

Jerks are "bugs in fruit."

So what do we do about it?

Focus on the *fruit*. Not the bugs.

* * *

Here's the *rub*.

The bugs get *so* much more attention than they deserve.

If we don't watch out, we'll forget the fruit's even there—because we're too busy thinking about the bugs.

We gotta just wipe 'em off and send 'em right down the garbage disposal—and move *on*.

Stories about the jerks are all over the national news, the city news, the town news, in the chit-chat on the pickleball court. So much energy, so much bandwidth yapping about the "bugs in fruit."

The other day, on the "Next Door" app, a guy wrote about how he was parked at the grocery store in town, and three 'teens' on scooters called him a "Bozo."

Seventy-eight people. Seventy-eight people wrote comments, mostly under the theme of the *Bye Bye Birdie* song, *What's the Matter with Kids Today?*

Couple things.

If the worst thing that happened to me today was a couple knucklehead kids called me a "Bozo"—that would be one *great* day.

I'd tell 'em, "Thanks for the 'shout out.' One of my favorite shows growing up."

On top of that, to *them*, I *am* a Bozo.

Think about it. I'm *four* times their age. To them, I dress like Ben Franklin. And the longest hair on my head isn't as long as ones sprouting out of their nose.

Bozo.

Please. Tell me something I don't know.

Bugs in fruit.

Here's what I *do* know.

This morning, when I was walking my dog past the grocery store, a guy riding by on his bike stopped in the street to pick up a random plastic Coke bottle—and put it in a garbage can.

When I was in the store, Susie, a sweet pea in the bakery department, gave me a little chocolate gift to give my wife.

Whoops. Never made it home.

✳ ✳ ✳

So *what's* the fix? How do we stop focusing on the bugs?

How 'bout this.

Do like Will Ferrell said in that stupid movie where he coached the little girls' soccer team.

Do the *opposite*.

Once a day, make a point to do something just *wonderful*.

One little extra thing that makes the world just a little bit *better*.

That puts a smile on somebody's face. Puts a *snap* in their step.

Maybe in a restaurant, stick your head in the kitchen, look the cooks in their eyes, and tell 'em how *talented* they are.

Maybe go through your old pics. Find one of your brothers or sisters. Or an old pal. Email 'em how it reminded you how lucky you are that they're in your life.

That kind-of grumpy old lady on the block who lives alone? Always complaining about the gifts your dog leaves on her lawn?

Knock on her door. Hand her a flower from your backyard. In a little vase. Tell her it looks like her.

Stuff like that.

I'll bet, if you *do* that, you're going to really love something.

A one-of-a-kind piece of fruit.

The most delicious, beautiful, wondrous fruit in the whole world...

You.

A GENTLEMAN'S WORD

My flight was delayed in an airport, and I did something I'd never done.

I got a shoeshine.

As he began on one of my shoes, rather than just enjoy the simple ten-minute moment, I was lost on my iPhone, banging away at an endless drawer of emails.

I never even looked up.

As I was paying the gentleman after he finished, I disingenuously asked him how he was doing.

He looked deep into my eyes, smiled, and said…

One word.

* * *

Cut to the plane. With a battery-dead laptop, I had a wonderful, rare moment of time to do nothing but *think*.

Not about what was due tomorrow or what was coming up down the line—but I took a "time out" to wonder about his word.

We all know how time goes faster the higher up we are. Time's flying by right now at record speed.

Maybe *that's* the trick.

To get closer to the ground. To feel the heartbeat of the earth. To listen to what's close by—and to listen for things far away that we've forgotten to even hear at all.

And, maybe, just maybe—we'll hear that gentleman's word. That beautiful word. Maybe the most beautiful word of all…

Grateful.

FAMILY

Fifty thousand years ago, ten thousand years ago, two thousand years ago, a hundred years ago, something has *always* been true.

We always lived in the same cave, the same hut, the same home, the same town with our tribes. Our families.

If we moved, we all packed up and moved *together*. That's how it worked.

It's been a powerful, rich, inspiring fabric of every generation back to the beginning.

In my family tree, there are more Irish Dunne relatives in the suburbs of Chicago than there are maple trees.

I love 'em all.

✳ ✳ ✳

Cut to 1970.

With trains, planes, and automobiles, *anywhere* became your oyster.

Young people in our generation, pretty much for the first time ever, were being pulled away—hearing a muse from a distant land.

Some for a career, some for the weather, some for love.

It was happening everywhere. With kids going out-of-state to colleges, the floodgates opened.

They moved away with a handful of bucks in their pockets and a collect phone number to call home—leaving everything and everyone in the rearview mirror.

For me, after college days, I packed up my part-car, part-tin-can bright yellow Mazda GLC with a one-way tank of gas, with all my stuff and all my dreams—and set the compass to California.

✳ ✳ ✳

Fast-forward a generation. Adding cell phones and the internet to the mix, more and more kids today are moving *everywhere*.

The planet is their canvas to work and play.

Compare this to my four grandparents. Not one of them ever got on a plane in their *lives*. I'd guess they probably never traveled more than two hundred miles from their hometowns.

I'm one of seven brothers and sisters—with twenty-one collective kids between us.

Of those twenty-one, not one lives in our hometown today. They're scattered throughout Pennsylvania, Maine, Florida, Tennessee, California, Ohio, Indiana, New York, Arizona, Oregon, Washington, and London.

* * *

A couple of weeks ago, five of our seven siblings were going to Glacier National Park for a few days.

I wasn't going to be able to make it. I was swamped with work. Not good timing. I'd see them another time.

It was days away, and I called my brother in Chicago, who also wasn't making the trip.

We decided we needed to change our plans and make it happen. We needed to get the seven of us together. It would be the first time we'd all be together since both our parents passed away.

I can't tell you how glad I am that I went.

We belly-laughed a million times, we cried at the drop of a hat, and we remembered where we came from.

We remembered the gift of our parents. How they selflessly gave up *so* much—just for *us*.

How they somehow made *each* one of us feel so special to them—and to the world.

And suddenly, those trivial spats over something a sister or brother said or did drifted a million miles away. *Who* cares.

At our dinner on the last night of the trip, my brother asked us if we'd share our favorite moments from the trip.

Some spoke about the hikes and bike rides together. And the majesty and the smell of the trees—and the *wonder* of the lakes and mountains in this breathtaking place.

The moment I shared was when my sister, Julie, was trying to slide out of her canoe on her rump onto the lake's pier—without flopping right in the drink.

We all were howling so hard as this poor young guy, working on the dock, was giving it everything he possibly had to yank her up onto that pier.

You just *can't* beat it.

Nothing in the world mattered in that beautiful moment, looking at my family. Thinking about my parents and how much they would have given *anything* to be right there, belly-laughing with the rest of us.

On the flight home from that trip, I looked out the window down at the earth far, far away.

I thought about those two powerful forces.

A gravitational one pulling to keep all the planets circling the sun, and another causing everything in the universe to distance itself from whatever it's near.

Being together. Hugs. Pats on the back from family truly *rooting* for you. Being in the moment. Looking into each other's eyes to find reflections of who you are and where you came from.

Don't be like me. Always just say *yes*.

Yes, to that most precious, fragile, one-of-a-kind treasure in the world...

Family.

CLUB SPORTS

There's something our generation made up—that's gotten out of control.

Club sports.

I want to find the guy who made up, "Let's have a ton of kids and parents get up at five on a Saturday morning, drive an hour and a half to some giant sweatbox in Anaheim so sixth graders can play seven games of volleyball against kids and teams they'll never see again."

Yesterday a pal was all pumped up, telling me how his four-year-old granddaughter was invited to join an *elite* gymnastics club. And bragging about how the walls are *lined* with posters of Olympian alumni.

Yikes.

At four, I was still wrestling with toilet training.

Seems to me what started out as an idea for gifted, cream-of-the-crop athletes playing against other truly extraordinary athletes has evolved, over the years, into casting a much, *much* wider net.

And the carrot many clubs are dangling in front of parents and kids?

College scholarships. Olympic dreams. Pro careers.

Many club websites are loaded up with case studies of how your kids' dreams are *sure* to come true.

As one of seven kids, my parents didn't see sports as a way to get college paid for. Sports was a way to get our butts *out* of the house.

* * *

I'll bet the ranch many of your journeys looked a lot like *this*.

I rode my bike in my uniform to a baseball league game at the park about ten blocks from my house. We played *one* game.

The game lasted an hour, not eight hours.

We played against pals we knew from school and town, and they were on teams with snappy names like "La Grange State Bank" and "Sauerberg Pharmacy."

There was a trendy brand of shoes *everyone* wore in our town. Called "gym shoes."

The only Nike I ever heard of was a winged knockout living large on a mountaintop in Greece.

Gym shoes were *fabulous* for baseball, basketball, tennis, touch football, and golf between the goalposts at the football field—and they were great in summer, winter, spring, and fall.

As you can see, they were a hell of a lot bigger than my foot, but I'm sure I grew into them in a couple years.

After we played, the dad coaches would treat us to a dip cone at Frosty Freeze. With a face and tummy full of happy and ice cream, we rode our second-hand bikes home.

During the summer, we played you-name-it at the park *without* coaches, parents, fielding, or batting specialists—for *hours*. Just hanging with my buddies goofing around. That's where I learned to play every sport. And a whole lot more in life.

And after baseball season ended, we all played football. And then we all played basketball. We also played tennis, swam, ice skated, and played golf or anything else that had balls, pucks, racquets, paddles, or scoring.

Whether you were great or stunk, you played in the same leagues and on the same teams. It didn't matter all that much. And if you stunk badly enough, you did something else.

✳ ✳ ✳

My parents' total investment in my nine-year baseball career was two mitts (one used), baseball cleats in my "sunset years," and some balls, bats, and cups. That's it.

And nobody, *nobody*, can convince me we didn't have just as much—or *more* fun as our kids committing thousands and thousands of hours to one sport (and a ton of parents' money) to keep up with every other club kid, coast to coast.

In general, are kids better baseball/hockey/basketball/volley-ball/soccer/tennis players today?

Yeah, they're better.

But *so* what.

Hip-hip hurray. The next generation of baseball players may decrease fielding errors by 2.67 percent.

Who wins? *Nobody.*

Not the kids. Not the parents. Nobody.

We all know it's in vogue to have/do "more." That "more is better." Super-sized fries. Five sets instead of three in tennis. More homework. More books in a kid's backpack. More pages to sign on "home loan" documents. More credit card. More botox. Six matches a day in volleyball tournaments instead of one.

All bad ideas.

The Kentucky Derby lasts two minutes.

That's why it's exciting. If it were an endurance contest where the horses ran around the track twenty times, I don't think there would be a mint julep.

✳ ✳ ✳

Kids' sports are like brooms and ropes.

When they're little squirts, we're the *broom*. We sweep 'em gently into sports and programs we think will be good for 'em.

But then it gets tricky.

They get *in* something. So do their friends. We blink, and *they* and *we* start chasing the carrot.

Little by little, the geography of games shifts from our *own* town backyard, to long car rides, then to plane rides on holiday weekends. Costs and time commitments blossom *exponentially.*

Sound familiar?

That's where the question of the *rope* kicks in.

You can't *push* a rope. But somebody is *always* pulling the rope, and somebody is *always* getting pulled along.

You have to ask yourself, deep down... *who's* pulling? Is it your *kid*? Is it *you*?

I'd make sure it's your *kid* who's doing the pulling.

And if they stop pulling, maybe it's time to give 'em the slack to put the rope away.

We all find it's in *those* moments—those hard, real moments—where love and respect live.

✳ ✳ ✳

I *do* know this.

Our kids only get one shot at growing up, and we only have one shot of watching them do it.

As Oscar Hammerstein said, "Life is a carousel, my friend; life is a carousel."

So true.

The ride is so much fun if it's at the right speed and lasts the right amount of time.

But it's no fun for *anybody* if it's spinning *too* fast—and you can't get *off*.

LEFTIES

I know you're not supposed to be prejudiced against any group of people, but I can't help myself with one group.

Lefties.

They're just *so* cool. I'm sure ten percent out there would agree.

They're just…

What's the word?

Better?

So fun to be with. What's not to *love* about a lefty?

And to all you righties, we know *deep* down that you're just a *little* bit jealous.

Beside us humans, some of my favorite animals in the whole-wide world are predominantly lefties. Duh. Kangaroos. Only the coolest animal in the southern hemisphere, Parrots. Left-footer all the way. You'll never look at the adorable lefty parrot the same way again! And, last but not least, toads. So underestimated. Spectacular harmonies.

We're good sports. We don't let the little stuff get to us.

Smearing ink all over our hands when we write, righty scissors, backward coffee cups, upside-down belts, watches, three-ringed binders, swiping credit cards, can openers, computer mouses—and *we're* not complaining.

* * *

And we've been taking a lot, and I mean a *lot*, of heat over the years.

Maybe it's true we're just a speck—I mean a *speck*—more absent-minded.

And we couldn't *care less* that "left" comes from the Old English "lyft"—meaning "weak," "useless," or "broken."

Or, in Latin, from "sinister"—or in German, from "awkward" or "clumsy."

In China, because being lefty was a sign of deviancy, children were forced to switch to their right hand. In many Muslim countries, the left hand is unclean, used for "toilet purposes." Offering anything with the left hand is just plain impolite and offensive.

Back in the day in Europe or America, when folks were on the prowl for witches in town, you wouldn't want them to find your set of lefty golf clubs.

Lefties feel really warm and cozy visiting Morocco and Algeria, where, not too long ago, you could be imprisoned for being a southpaw because you're a *s'ga*—a "devil" or "cursed person."

How *lovely*.

Speaking of devils—name any one of them. They're *100 percent* lefties.

Go figure.

There have been some cute names for lefties over the years.

Skivvy-handed, kaggy-fisted, mollydooker, scrummy-handed, cawk-fisted, cack-handed, libtard, and gibble-fisted.

I don't know what any of these mean, but I'm taking a wild guess they're not pump-you-up compliments.

Hmmm.

Leonardo da Vinci. Ruth Bader Ginsburg. Albert Einstein. Helen Keller. Pablo Picasso. Neil Armstrong. Michelangelo. Lewis Carroll. Paul McCartney. Bill Gates. Lady Gaga. Isaac Newton. Oprah. Aristotle. Tina Fey. Benjamin Franklin. Dr. Seuss. Beethoven. Mark Twain. Marie Curie. Charles Dickens. Babe Ruth. Jimi Hendrix. Rembrandt. Barack Obama. Paul Simon. Edward R. Murrow. Charlie Chaplin. Nikola Tesla. Ringo. Buzz Aldrin. Bart Simpson. Charles Darwin. Sting. Alan Turing. John Kennedy. Raphael. Bob Dylan. Gandhi.

Lyft *that*.

BEING A FATHER

*F*or birthdays, holidays, Father's Day, you name it, ask any dad. We don't want our kids spending money on any presents for us. We just want the cards. Something where they tell us that a little bit of us—is a little bit of them.

Gifts—we don't need. We've got plenty. That's what Amazon is for.

But what we can't buy on Father's Day is what it means to have our kids in a room looking at us in the eyes—or feeling their hearts beating through a phone from across the country.

New to the job of being a grampie, I love watching my kids' pals cruising around with their strollers and dangling their toes in the amazing waters of being parents.

A few thoughts for the young dads out there…

***

Being a father.

Going in, I had no idea how to be a good one—and I feel like I know even *less* now. I've made thousands of mistakes raising our two girls so far, and I'm sure today will be no exception.

But I can tell you *this*.

Having a kid took about ten minutes—and that's if you include brushing my teeth, turning on the music, and kicking the dog off the bed.

Becoming a father is something I've been working at every single day since my wife looked me in the eyes and said, "We're having a baby."

As their lives keep twisting and turning, I'm hanging on for dear life to one of the most treasured, glorious, inspiring, rich roles in my journey here on this earth…

Being a father.

***

And if you think it's all going by fast now, buckle in for the *fastest* ride in your life.

I was *you* fifteen minutes ago.

And, trust me, along every step of the journey, gravity will be pulling you into meetings, into golf games, into your texts and emails, you name it.

Here's my old-man advice.

Whenever you start feeling sorry for yourself and wishing you were somewhere else, imagine you're sixty-seven. When you'd give your left arm to be able to go back and spend five minutes with them, just *one* more time.

And here's *why*.

You can't go back.

You can't go back to the feeling of holding them, only *minutes* old—and welcoming them into the world.

To witnessing your wife holding her baby for the very first time.

To the joy of feeding them in their high chairs, driving 'em with their helmets on the back of your bike, or reading to them in their beds, gently tucked under your arm.

To seeing your kids charge down the stairs at Christmas.

Or to standing in the back of an auditorium watching 'em sing or dance in a school play, or to cheering on the sidelines when they're baby horses just trying their best to stand up in front of their friends.

I'm not saying it's *all* pretty. No doubt about it: it *is* a roller coaster—with unbearable turns when you just can't wait for the track to straighten out.

* * *

You think you're losing sleep when your kid is just a few months old?

Just wait until you're in the back half of high school years. Or when your kids are home for summers in college.

Tell me how *that* feels, waiting up all night long for them to come strolling in the door.

But I can promise you *this*.

As they evolve, so will *you*. You will become a father and a man who does the *right* thing when the moment calls.

You're going to know the meaning of a word that's the *biggest* word in the world.

A word that has *so* many dimensions. So complicated. So rich. So awesome. So beautiful. So terrifying. A word that makes you so profoundly full.

Love.

And as days and years march on, it just gets better and better.

But the bonus to *me*? I thought the ride ended after college.

Nope.

You're *still* on the team. You just don't get to play as much.

They *still* want and need a dad. A voice of reason. Of balance. Of integrity. Of honor. Of discipline. Who champions the *wonder* of it all.

Maybe not *every* day, but when they call, what a thrill it is to come in off the bench to get in their game.

✳ ✳ ✳

Give yourself a treat tonight before you go to bed.

Look in the mirror. Take a *good* long look.

And see in that mirror the generations before you—who would be *so* proud of the man you have become.

And give thanks for the greatest gift you could ever imagine.

The privilege of belonging to that sacred, honorable fraternity.

Being a *father*.

THROW IT OUT OF BOUNDS

The other day, at an event at SoFi Stadium, I had the chance to go out on the field.

And *dream*.

Dream of how our Rams must have felt. Two minutes to go in the Super Bowl. Stafford finds Kupp heroically marching down the field. I could *hear* the seventy thousand in the crowd.

And then I thought of *my* football career.

Not so much the same.

It peaked, if you'd want to call it that, when I was in eighth grade.

St. Francis Falcons. Our Catholic grammar school team in La Grange, Illinois.

Those autumn Sunday games would be absolutely *packed*.

As a little kid at St. Francis, you dreamed of *someday* running through the huge banner held out by the cutest cheerleaders. Just roaring across the field to a *sea* of St. Francis fans cheering on their Falcon warriors.

I played left halfback. I had *one* move. That's it.

I didn't care what play the quarterback called.

If I got the ball, I was grabbing that thing and going "left." Heading straight to the left sideline and then doing my move. The "stiff arm."

The goal of my play was to end up still standing up.

The other end of the spectrum? What *hell* looked like. Running straight up the middle.

Get slaughtered and end up at the bottom of a big pile of giant, goat-smelling friends.

✳ ✳ ✳

It was a pre-season summer practice—in a record-squelching August.

Smack in the middle of the afternoon on that practice field; it felt more like the top of a barbecue grill than a park. About 250°F—with no wind, and I'm pretty sure the "Woodstock" for flying bugs.

My football scouting report wasn't exactly "peaking" after my less-than-stellar seventh-grade season.

In seventh grade, they demoted me to the sixth-grade team. *That* makes you feel *really* cool inside.

And to rub a bucket of vinegar in my wounds, my younger brother (who *was* in sixth grade) played on the eighth-grade team.

Didn't help very much in the potential girlfriend department, either.

Back to that eighth-grade practice.

After a few practices, the coaches had pretty much set in stone that I (and this other kid on the team, Rick Carney) were the runts of the litter.

Carney lived right behind our house, so we were best buddies growing up.

Now that I think about it, maybe Carney and I should have spent a little more time running around the block instead of on our walkie-talkie wires that ran from my house to his.

Carney and I got the hint that the coaches weren't *exactly* drinking the Kool-Aid of our amazing potential—when they dished out our practice uniforms.

They ran out of football jerseys for everybody, so Carney and I just wore undershirts over our shoulder pads. When we'd run, we'd be like flapping geese with the shoulder pads bouncing and clacking around.

But the kicker was the helmets.

They didn't have any "regular" helmets for both of us—you know, the kind with facemasks to protect you.

They gave Carney and me the used, *reject* helmets from the old Pop Warner league in town.

Those were the kind Knute Rockne wore back in the thirties.

No facemask. Just this decades-old, hand-me-down, brown leather thing Carney and I stuck on our heads.

But my problem was my helmet (if you'd want to call it that) didn't really fit on my big head.

I found if I wore the thing *backward*, it was a little snugger.

So I did *that*.

The only problem was, sometimes the thing would flop down in front of my eyes when I was running. But you do what you gotta do.

It was the start of practice, all melting in the heat. Carney and I were standing around the coach, looking like absolute dopes in our caveman helmets. The coach told everybody to do the same thing we did at the start of every practice.

Four laps around the goalposts.

Off we all went.

That's fun.

By the end of the first lap, Carney and I were *already* exhausted, chugging along in our spots of last and next-to-last place. Only Carney was behind me.

I was heading down the field for lap two—now only fifty yards away from those white, wooden goalposts—where everybody else had already made the turn.

I had to stay positive, one step at a time.

Just kept picturing and dreaming about all my favorite cheerleaders who barely knew my name—Cathy Malec, Peggy Baker, Madelyn Giloth, Kathy Powers—*wildly* cheering as I'd be busting through that banner on the first game only a month away.

I wiped off the mosquitoes snacking on my face, let those shoulder pads bounce around under my Fruit of the Loom, and *charged* down that field.

Only three yards from the goalpost. Making the turn.

I figured no point in running one extra foot if I didn't have to. So I'd cut it close around that goal post like a downhill skier.

What I *didn't* count on was the helmet flopping in front of my eyes.

Next thing I knew, I plowed right into that goalpost.

And down I went.

Flat on my back with my arms spread out. Out cold.

And I know this sounds like something that would happen in a cartoon, but I swear to God, my Knute Rockne helmet snapped in two—right down the middle.

The helmet looked like a cracked eggshell next to my head, and I was like a sizzling patty on the Memorial Park griddle.

Next thing I knew, I came to, looking up at the whole team of St. Francis players.

Coach Pridmore looked down at me and asked, "Dunne, do you know what day it is?"

I looked up at my teammates.

I looked over at the two halves of my helmet. I said, "The last day of my football career."

✳ ✳ ✳

Fast-forward to the first game of the season. I had a new role on the team.

Announcer.

Stood on top of this two-story scaffolding with a mic and called the play-by-play.

The fans loved me.

Couldn't have been *better*.

A few years later, I wrote their "St. Francis Fight Song" with my brother. All the moms and dads, cheerleaders, and kids still sing it today at all their games.

Here's the lesson I learned.

So what.

So what if I'm not a professional football player.

Last time I checked, none of those guys on that team ever were *either*.

Sometimes, in football, the best move you can make is to throw it out of bounds.

Cut your losses.

Take a breath.

Think of a better play—and do *that*.

MONET'S GARDEN

Like a bird that flies south and may not know why it's doing it, I often find myself on a plane to SMU in Dallas in the late spring.

About a decade ago, at my daughters' college campus, I started a tradition for the seniors in the same fraternity house from my college days.

"Senior Night" has evolved into a yearly tradition where about fifty seniors and their dads have a dressed-up dinner a few days before the university's graduation.

* * *

Every year, it's the same rhythm.

A quiet, elegant room in a private dinner club. Each senior stands up during dinner and makes a toast to "who they were, who they are, and where they're going."

For many of the seniors and dads, it's *very* emotional. Many express things in that moment they may have *never* said to their friends—or to their dad.

* * *

In the "cool down" drink after the event, a senior thanked me for "mc-ing" this event and asked a simple question, "You don't have a son in this fraternity, and you fly down here to do this for a bunch of strangers? How come?"

I'm sure I said something brilliant like, "Because you guys are the *greatest*," with an idiot grin on my face and probably gave him the fraternity "grip."

So here I am, sitting on the plane heading back to California, thinking about what the answer should have been.

I think I go there to fill a bit of a hole in my soul.

When I graduated from U. of Kentucky, I had no interest in sitting on the thirty-six yard-line with 6,765 other graduates in rented costumes listening to somebody I never heard of yakking about how I should reach for my dreams.

So, a couple of days earlier, I just hopped in my piss-yellow, rusty-old Mazda GLC with a zillion miles and memories...

And drove away.

I drove away from the home of so many incredible buddies who shared a rich, wild, and full ride of college life.

I drove away from a girlfriend who taught me about how spectacular it is to love someone—and for someone to love you back.

I drove away from a place that was a bottomless treasure chest of learning that ripped open my mind to the wonders of science, literature, and the arts.

The gears were shifting down as I went from shoving my life in that clunker car, to backing out of my fraternity house driveway, to passing my university out the car window—to smelling and tasting and hearing the green grass whistling in the wind under the white-picket fences of my old Kentucky home horse farms.

✳ ✳ ✳

As the farms disappeared and as I merged onto the highway, it emotionally hit me. I didn't know why I was so overcome, but I knew something was profoundly shifting in my journey.

By the time I drove into my hometown eight hours later in La Grange, Illinois, I had cut the umbilical cord from my childhood—and found myself being swept up in the air of an arctic stream that would carry me to my adventure in California.

✳ ✳ ✳

Back to the answer to the question the kid asked me.

I suppose it's because I didn't have a definitive moment to let go of my college relationships, and I hoped this event would provide that for these young men and their dads.

I do think there's value in definitively letting go of things, forcing you to stretch out for new branches and see if they can support you—when, oftentimes, you don't even know those branches were *there*.

I suppose it's because I believe saying goodbye to places and people and experiences are nature's first steps, mortality's baby steps, to subtly prepare us for ultimately saying goodbye to life.

First steps to letting go of this amazing, complicated, fun, painful, exciting, symphony of life where we're so blessed to be momentarily holding the baton as a guest conductor.

If we take the time to recognize endings along the way, and if we're willing to emotionally digest the fragility, pain, and humility in these moments, maybe we're tasting truths about who we were, who we are, and where we think we're going.

My feeling is that no matter what we're saying goodbye to—whether it's an important relationship, a chapter in our lives, or a tie that's had its days—on some level, we're yanked out of the race of the day to appreciate how nice the trip has been.

When we say goodbye to a tie, we're not saying goodbye to the *tie*.

But to who we were when we wore it.

* * *

It reminds me of standing on the bridge in Monet's backyard in Giverny, France.

I had read about his perspective on what he tried to draw.

He was fascinated with how the rays of light between our eyes and an image is what we actually "see"—and how what we *see* has little to do with what the image actually *is*.

He drew the same images over and over again because he *wasn't* painting the image—he was drawing the rays of light he was seeing in that *moment*.

I suppose we do that naturally when we look at old college pictures or ties—or urns.

Maybe that's what I should have told the kid.

That I'm trying to draw rays of light.

Those kaleidoscopic, evocative, wondrous rays of light.

CADDY DAYS

I just got back from playing golf. Snappy club, snappy caddies, snappy everything.

On the eighteenth green, I handed my caddy $140.

As I forked over a wad of twenties, I flashed back to *my* caddy days.

$4.75 and a "caddy special" hot dog.

At La Grange Country Club. A lovely club in my hometown.

Let's back up a second.

* * *

I still hold two records in my town as a kid.

One, as a pitcher in Little League—for beaning twenty-two batters in a single season.

That's a pretty good aim when you consider I only got to pitch six games in a season with six-inning games.

And some of the games, they pulled me out because I had *already* beaned (or scared) too many kids.

I stunk as a pitcher, but let's just say I put the fear of God in anybody stepping in that batter's box.

The other record is for being the "worst all-time caddy at La Grange Country Club."

In my rookie caddy season in sixth grade, I started like every kid in my town—as a "shagger."

Our driving range was only about 150 yards, and in those days, golfers had their own bag of "shag balls."

As a "shagger," you'd stand out in the driving range with a catcher's face mask and baseball glove and catch the guy's iron shots he was aiming at you.

I was shagging for Sandy Austin. A nice, dapper, short guy. Crazy rich. Owned a bank downtown. Even his shag balls were brand-new Titleists.

Since I was making only $1.65 as a shagger, I decided to make up a rule standing out there like a big dope in that itchy catcher's face mask.

The first ball I'd catch would go in his shag bag. The next ball—right into my shorts' pockets.

I figured it was kind of like a mandatory "tip." One ball for him, one for me until my pants were stuffed.

The problem was I got a little greedy that day. I ran out of room in my pockets. Started shoving 'em up in my underpants.

After an hour of shagging, you'd carry the guy's clubs to the cement floor bag room. As he was standing next to me signing the chit for my whopping $1.65, I bent over to set down his bag.

About five golf balls with his name on 'em snuck out of my underwear and started bouncing up and down on the cement.

Whoops.

I got a couple of months of "hiatus" after that lovely stunt.

Who cares.

It was rookie year. On to being a real caddy in seventh grade.

✳ ✳ ✳

I had a number of legendary stories to earn the title of "worst all-time caddy," but here's one of my personal favorites.

Scorching hot, I mean a *scorching* hot, muggy August day. Mosquitoes enjoying full-course meals on your neck, arms, and legs.

Caddying for J. C. Kenter. A big ole, tightwad grump. Spongy gut hung over his embroidered country club-logoed belt.

He thought my name was "Caddy."

That morning, the club just got brand-new golf carts.

The fancy kind that didn't steer like go-carts—they steered like a car. You had to turn the wheel a lot more to head in a direction.

It was *totally* against the rules to let a caddy *ever* get in the carts. You just ran after the thing like a big goof and then handed 'em their clubs.

Cut to the fifteenth hole's green. Dizzy-long par four. Sun sizzling everyone—with sweat soaking everyone's shirts and patience.

With the foursome getting ready to putt, I reached into J. C. Kenter's bag to get his putter, and realized I committed a mortal sin.

I left his putter back on the green of the last hole. About a Sahara Desert away.

Let's just say those four dripping, liquored-up golfers weren't real happy campers.

J. C. screamed a whole long laundry list of very colorful adjectives that he decided described me—and then half threw up his roast beef sandwich as he pointed for me to get in the damn cart, get the putter, and bring it back.

I hopped on that horse and gunned it straight down the fairway.

Pulled right up to the side of the lake next to the previous green—with a lovely pitched, brick embankment around the water's edge.

Kind of looked like this.

Ran over, grabbed the putter off the green, and threw it in the cart.

Here's where things kind of started falling apart.

I forgot the carts didn't steer like go-carts anymore.

Turned the wheel, gunned it, and the next thing I knew, it was down the embankment—and *most* of me and *most* of the cart were underwater.

I put it in reverse with the wheels spinning and splashing—and got in the water, trying to shove the thing back up the embankment.

Good luck with *that* one.

All the cart did was puke *buckets* of mud on my soaked face.

Hopped out of the cart, grabbed his putter, and ran as fast as I could down the fairway like a sopping wet, black-faced goose.

THE MOMENT BEFORE A SUNSET

Every once in a blue moon, we're privileged to witness something.

Something that we unexpectedly find that *moves* us.

That inspires us. That shapes us.

One of those happened to me this morning.

It wasn't a grand speech by a national leader; it wasn't an astounding film or television show.

It was something right in my own town's backyard.

It was a third-grade musical at a grade school in town.

It wasn't the quality of their singing, or intricate dance steps, or great lighting or sound. None of that.

It was in a second-floor, most-of-the-time classroom—absolutely jam-packed with parents there to watch their kids.

Many of the moms and dads, heading off to their work or home offices right after the musical, were peeking down at their chirping phones—pulling them far away from that room.

Then, out on the stage, twenty kids appeared. All spread out. Like chess pieces on a chessboard. Twenty of the most beautiful, unique faces you could ever imagine. All scanning the room for the loving blanket of their parents.

There is just *something* about that age. That five-to-nine-year-old, once-in-a-lifetime sweet spot, where they don't think much about tomorrow, and they don't think much about yesterday.

They're in the *right now*.

They hear, and they see, and they feel *everything* in the now.

It's that treasured small window of our life's journey where we're shooting stars with incandescent light.

The intro of the music came from a rusty, out-of-tune upright piano off the side of the stage. Then something absolutely *marvelous* happened.

They *sang*.

They sang in a tone and a style and a voice so pure, so real, so emotional that no pop singer could compare.

As the kids looked out at all of us, we were swept away. What *they* were feeling, *we* were feeling.

For all of us adults in that room, the politics and divisiveness of the news, anything—was suddenly *gone*. All those things that wander into your head—about checkbook balances, health issues, stress about careers—weren't in the room.

Everyone was just *there*. Just *there*.

When the final song finished, and with everyone in the room singing along, the parents cheered. They cheered, and they cheered, and they cheered.

They cheered for who their kids were, who they are, and who they *dream* to be.

They cheered for the wonder of that muse that whispers in the ear of a child to trust their own voice.

They cheered for the privilege of sharing that moment with their friends from their parish who will be a part of their lives and their stories *forever*.

I watched the parents finding their third-grader in the stir and the joy of the "backstage" celebration.

With no words, they hugged their kids a bit longer, trying to hold on to this moment just a little more.

⁂

Sunsets.

Many of my pals just can't get enough of 'em. I'm not really a sunset guy.

The moment I love happens somewhere in the time just *before* that. It doesn't have a name that I know of.

It's that maybe seven-minute window when the sun brushes over the water, transforming it into this kind of aqua blue that can't *possibly* have a word that describes its beauty.

It's *more* than any color. It's a *feeling*.

And at that moment, the sun illuminates every face, every thing. The lapping water on the sand paints momentary masterpieces. The white cusps of the waves frost the warm sea. The islands and mountains in the distance *sing*.

And then, in just an instant, it goes away.

The sky darkens just a bit as the earth spins just enough to lose sight of its mothering sun.

* * *

Back to our story.

Along with all the parents in that room, I walked down the flight of stairs, through the piazza of the school, and to the parking lot.

As we headed to our cars, like the shifting sky, all the tasks and all the worries of the day seeped their way back smack to center stage. My phone buzzed and beeped, reeling me, like a fisherman, right back on the hook.

No matter what, I'm going to visit the beach tonight before sunset.

To see it *again*.

And, at that moment, I'm going to give thanks for what I saw today. For what I was privileged to *feel*. For the gift I was given by those children.

I'll imagine those parents tonight, looking across the dinner table at their third graders talking about their day.

And I'll give thanks for how lucky I am to live in such a beautiful town where flowers like these have such a chance to bloom.

With a color too beautiful to even have a name.

THE BARBERSHOP

I took a walk this morning into town.

I don't know if I'd call it a *walk*; I was multitasking on my phone, yakking away through the mic in my earbuds while, at the same time, knocking down as many emails as I could on that iPhone screen.

I don't even know if I knew where I was walking. How I got through crosswalks without even looking up was a miracle.

I walked by the Palisades Barber Shop. I remembered my nagging phone's to-do list said I was overdue for a haircut.

I stepped inside. One of the town's favorites, owner Joe Almaraz, invited me to put my phone away and hop in his too-comfy chair.

I took a breath as I sunk in that chair and as he wrapped me in a haircut bib.

✳ ✳ ✳

Joe's been the barber there for fifty-nine years. He walks to work every day from his home in town. It's a "family business," where the next chairs over are for his daughter-in-law Lucy, Lucy's husband JR, and Joe's son Tony.

I'd describe the interior design style of the barbershop as "late sixties." Lots of wood paneling. A flat-screen TV on the wall (that only plays Dodgers games) is the only "tell" that Hoss Cartwright from *Bonanza* isn't likely to walk in.

While you get a cut in Joe's chair, you can't help noticing that every single person who walks by the storefront window smiles and waves to their favorite barber.

You don't have to tell Joe what kind of cut you want. He *knows*.

And you're not going to see what your head looks like until he's done, and he spins you around to look in his hand mirror.

But when you *do* look, you always feel a little cleaner. A little better.

About your head and about your heart.

We covered a lot of ground while Joe snipped away. I don't have a lot to cut. I think he pretends he's snipping half the time just so we can have a nice chat.

And don't let his "aw shucks" air fool you. He's had everyone in that chair—from Elon Musk, to Tom Hanks, to Buzz Aldrin, to Vin Scully, to Billy Bob Thornton, and every politician and celebrity and bigshot in between.

A theme Joe likes to talk about is that he's drawn to the "good old days." Of our town. Of America. Of life. Days of family-owned, mom-and-pops in town. Days when phones were plugged into the wall and when you couldn't leave a message.

Days when "streaming" had to do with catching a tasty fish.

And the more Joe talks in that calm, relaxed voice, the deeper you drift back into that bottomless chair and into a hypnotized daze of "way back when."

And then Joe takes off your bib, and up and out you go. It's not just the bright lights that smack you when you walk outside—it's the buzz of the street that snaps you back.

✳ ✳ ✳

Here's my takeaway.

The world's moving fast, and you gotta keep up. You gotta pay attention. If you don't, you spin right off the merry-go-round, and there's nobody there to catch you.

But let's call it what it is. The merry-go-round *is* fun. It's exciting.

And I really do *love* it. And lots of days, I really don't *want* to get off.

But, from now on, when I *do* get off, I'm going to look for a *chair*.

Maybe on a friend's front porch who I haven't seen in a while. Maybe a stump on a walk in the canyon. Maybe in a chair I never knew was even there in my own home.

And when I get up from that chair, I'm gonna look in a mirror.

That mirror may be in the eyes of a friend. Or in the river on the creek along the trail. Or in the laughter of my wife.

And who knows who I'll see in that mirror. But I'm going to guess I'm gonna feel a little cleaner. A little better.

About my head—and about my heart.

TROPHIES

I was at a meeting for a kids' sports conference—where a few folks brought up that maybe it's time to pull back on the gazillion trophies given out at every kids' sporting event.

We kicked around how kids are being weaned to expect to bring home some "hardware"—just for showing up.

Giving trophies out like water makes them unimportant when you finally get one that you *actually* deserve.

I was sitting there thinking about a trophy that I'll never toss out.

✳ ✳ ✳

It's a plastic six-inch gem I won the summer after my sophomore year in high school.

It maybe, maybe cost a quarter.

I won the sixteen-and-under golf tournament at Shady Shores Resort at Dewey Lake; I'm sure you've never heard of the place.

They ran out of golf trophies that year, so I got one with a shuffleboard player on it instead. Couldn't care *less*.

Adds a little mystery to this relic.

Dewey Lake was a brown shallow lake in the pancreas of Michigan that was so small you could swim across it (if you could stomach the god-only-knows-what growing in that lake rubbing against your legs).

It was, *no* doubt about it, the single greatest place on planet Earth.

Our fantastic kids' daily twelve-inch softball game with Mr. Murray. The morning game, then swimming out to the raft? Life doesn't get better.

* * *

Cut to the last night of our two-week family vacation—the infamous "Friday Night Bingo" and "Shady Shores Awards Ceremony" to a jam-packed lodge full of happy Midwestern families.

I couldn't even hear the bingo numbers being called out because I was so busy dreaming about how, in just *minutes*, I'd be parading up to the mic to absolutely *thunderous* applause.

Here's my younger brother, Terry, winning a cherry soda for a strong bingo hand. You can't see the huge crowd stuffed into the air-conditioning-less lodge. You can probably spot the lizard-sized mosquitoes sneaking in the windows for tasty summer hors d'oeuvres.

✳ ✳ ✳

And I was imagining the *amazing* things Resort Director Mr. Murray was going to say about me as he handed me my trophy in front of all my Dewey Lake pals, my family, and Sandy Roth from Cleveland, Ohio.

She was only the hottest freshman blond to ever, ever, ever vacation at Dewey Lake. She was the Grace Kelly of Shady Shores Resort.

It was the moment of truth.

Mr. Murray called my name.

As I proudly waved to my fans, heading to the front through the crowd of families, I *slammed* my face into a thick pea-green pillar.

It felt like Muhammad Ali just plowed me with a right hook. I plopped back into Mrs. O'Shanahan's ample lap.

As I waddled up to Mr. Murray in a daze, blood and mojo streamed down my face—and a knot the size of a grenade was ticking every second on my zitted forehead.

The whole place—my parents, my pals, and Sandy Roth— laughed their butts off, and Mr. Murray suddenly decided to become Dewey Lake's Don Rickles.

Maybe *that's* why I love that trophy.

Maybe because it's a bit of a snapshot of life at that moment.

Or maybe it's because winning that trophy kind of made up for the sting of losing in tennis a week before to a jackass, middle-aged town dad in the La Grange Tennis Tournament who hooked me on a key line call—just because he couldn't deal with the fact his tennis game and youth had long left the suburban train station.

Or maybe I love that trophy because I remember how I was still mending from getting totally dumped by my fabulously stacked high school girlfriend, who was a football field better looking and faster than me.

Maybe because it took my mind off thinking about the secret I was keeping from my mom and dad that my turd-brown used Schwinn bike got swiped from the caddy shack a couple days before we left for family vacation. Like a big dope, I didn't lock the thing, and I knew one of the older greaser caddies laughed the whole way home to Hopkins with a ciggie hanging off his chapped, ugly lips.

I'd be out of a bike for a couple months until I earned enough to buy another used beauty.

Or maybe I love that trophy because it reconnects me to that moment in time, that sweet moment in time, of early *dreams*.

Of hope. Of passion. Of wonder.

That trophy may look like an old plastic piece of nothing to anybody else—but to *me*, it's filled to the absolute brim with the fantastic and rich goop life, at its *finest*, is made of.

✳ ✳ ✳

If you get a moment, dig around your attic and pull out a trophy of yours that's been tucked away in some old, dusty box.

Let it *speak* to you. Let it *take* you there.

And see what pours out of the cup.

And then tuck it with the most tender care back in its box.

ROLLER COASTERS

A number of pals have recently got some really bad news about their health, or were in a bad accident, or lost someone unexpectedly in their lives.

Here's what's been remarkable.

How they *dealt* with it.

And I'm not talking about how they dealt with it at the moment they heard the news.

I'm talking about how they decided to move forward after the news settled in.

Here's one of them.

Last night, I was sipping cocktails with a buddy about ten yards away from the edge of the Pacific Ocean and watching our life-giving sun slip out of sight beyond the sea.

He shared that he had a colon operation last week. And how it was the fifth one he's had in the past few months.

He never told me.

Maybe *that's* why I'm writing this article. It just hit me over the head.

I know it was more than a routine "colon operation." But his take was, "So what? It's a great day *today*. It's been a fantastic journey up until now. How lucky am I."

* * *

Another pal, after surgeries putting seven plates in his face, is on operation number nine to his back, legs, lungs, and shoulders after a freak golf cart accident. He was launched out of the cart and crashed on his face and back.

He has been *nothing* but positive. Driven to heal.

Add to the mix a fantastic, selfless, and loving wife. He talks about how much it makes him appreciative of *everything* he has.

And I *know* a good part of the reason he has so miraculously healed is *because* of his attitude.

I'd bet you have friends in your life *just* like this.

What brave, heroic, inspiring ways to look at the amazing journey we're all privileged to take.

As with *so* many things, the dearest people in our lives are often our most inspiring and important teachers.

* * *

Jack Nicklaus talked about how he loved hearing some golfer on the practice tee at a tournament whining about the conditions of the course and how "it wasn't fair."

Like it wasn't *fair* for all the other players, too.

Jack said he could cross the guy off the list of having *any* prayer of winning.

The guy had *already* given himself an excuse to fail—before he even teed off.

Whining. It's the morphine of dreams.

⁎ ⁎ ⁎

Here's what I know.

I hit the lottery the day I was *born*.

I was healthy, in a fantastic family, in a great town, in the greatest country on the planet.

What in the *world* do I have to complain about?

I'm guessing it may be your story, too.

Yet, it's astounding how, in the day-to-day of it all, it's so easy for all of us to lose perspective. To find some kind of comfort in the "poor me."

We all wrestle with it.

I suppose life is kind of like a roller coaster.

You head up the big hill, wondering what's ahead and what's going to be just around the corner.

It's nonstop, and it's so great. It's exciting, so exhilarating, so fun, with amazing moments that just take your *breath* away.

But you better hold on because it's *going to* have some bumps and turns.

But, hopefully, as the ride slows down and you pull into that station, you look back and say...

"That was one *fantastic* ride."

MARTY'S FISH

My younger brother Marty lives in a Midwest prairie-style home in La Grange, Illinois, with his fabulous family—in the same house I grew up in.

Marty is truly one of my favorite human beings ever made.

Absolutely bursting with joy.

He turned his basement, the size of a tennis court, into a full-out zoo.

Chickens, ducks, a million birds, a miniature horse, the cutest big pig, skunks, whopper turtles, roosters, a lake full of fish…

You name it—it's flying around, swimming around, or trotting around his happy house and backyard.

Buses full of classes of kids show up at their house to go to his "zoo."

Every animal is named after somebody he loves. When he walks into the zoo, the animals pile on his arms and head.

He called this morning all pumped up—he just built a fabulous little aquarium on his kitchen table.

He said, "What I'm so excited about, I didn't make the thing to make *me* happy—I made it to make the *fish* happy."

One of the greatest thoughts I have *ever* heard a person say.

What a way to look at life.

At business. At family. At friends. At community.

Make the fish happy.

I'm so lucky to be a fish in Marty's beautiful aquarium.

THE ALIEN'S VISIT

It was my daughter Kaitlyn's thirteenth birthday, and she wanted to do something fun for her sleepover birthday party that night.

So her godfather, Ted McGinley, and I came up with our own Palisades version of Orson Welles's *War of the Worlds*.

Here's a blow-by-blow of that night…

7:50 PM

With Kaitlyn's six besties watching TV in our family room, Ted stopped by with a present for his goddaughter.

He nonchalantly asked if we had heard about the four "life forms" (as the news was calling them) who were captured a couple of hours ago on an asparagus farm near Fresno, California.

He said the Fresno authorities didn't know if there were more of 'em out there.

Ted had some cockamamie story about how the aliens were flown by fighter pilots to be nationally quarantined in Bethesda, Maryland.

8:05 PM

We had one of the moms call her daughter—and tell her not to be frightened about the Fresno incident. She wanted to let her daughter know that no matter *what* happened tonight, she'd always love her.

Let's just say *that* knocked things up a *big* notch.

8:10 PM

To take their minds off it, I stood right in front of the French doors that opened to our backyard—and showed the girls a new stupid juggling trick.

While I was doing the trick, Ted completely, I mean *completely*, covered from head to foot in Reynolds wrap—ran by in the backyard.

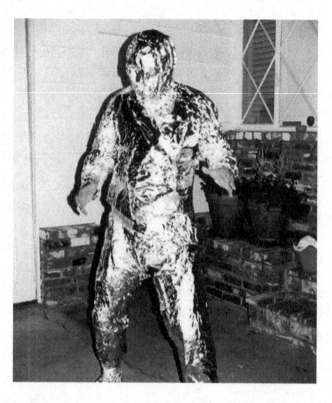

The "alien" had a quirky limp and made a high-pitched noise.

The girls *erupted*.

I became a tree—with every girl hanging on my body for dear life.

I told them their imaginations were getting the best of them—and that I didn't see anything run by.

They smelled that I was up to something, but they were loving the scary ride.

8:15 PM

We decided to call the police and report the incident. Whoops, my phone was dead. That's *odd*.

Yikes. The lights in the family room were flickering on and off. (Maybe that's because my wife, Catherine, had her back against the switch.)

We decided to all get in my Explorer and drive to the Palisades Police Station.

With a swarm of girls hanging on me, we walked, inch by inch, through the house and to the car.

8:20 PM

We carefully drove down our side street.

Out of *nowhere*, who jumped in front of our car—but the *alien*. The light shining on the Reynolds wrap made the alien look like a ball of white, sizzling energy.

Let's just say I *wish* I had earplugs.

8:25 PM

Arrived at the police station. I instructed the looney tunes to control themselves. I told 'em to have one girl tell the officer calmly what they thought they saw.

They all started yapping a million miles an hour.

The officer, a great guy, said the police station had received *numerous* sightings.

He handed them a flyer he said officers were currently distributing to every store and home in Pacific Palisades, warning them of the *imminent* danger.

He asked one of the girls to read the flyer out loud.

The kids were glued to Katie's friend Ashley Palmer, reading the three things you must do if you encounter an alien:

1. Take shelter in the nearest home.

2. Contact the Police Department.

3. Wish Kaitlyn a happy birthday—because she's just "out of this world."

THE ART OF TRAVELING

7,500 steps a day. That's a New Year's resolution I'm still kind of doing.

Louis, my dog, comes with me. The walks are doing him good. He's down a pound. That's one-eighth of his body weight.

I'll have to lose a leg to slice off one-eighth of my body weight.

I keep telling myself to *keep* going.

Get to the goal line of the bluffs overlooking the ocean. Those *beautiful* bluffs.

* * *

While walking along, an Instagram post popped up on my screen of a buddy on his "Which country should I visit *this* month?" trip to Antarctica. Standing next to a penguin on the shores of the beach.

I was thinking about how the closest I've been to one of the poles is dressing up in a Santa suit.

Never climbed a mountain that didn't have a comfy chairlift.

I not only haven't "sailed the seven seas," I can barely stand up on a paddleboard.

Ireland. My *motherland*. I'm hearing "My Wild Irish Rose."

The closest my body has been to Ireland is rubbing an Irish Spring Speed Stick in my armpit.

Hunting trips for moose, ducks, grizzly bears? Nope. Never shot anything that wasn't in my camera.

195 countries in the world. 186 to go.

* * *

I was pouting about how the clock was ticking and thinking about all the places I was *dying* to see.

Africa. New Zealand. Iceland. The Guadalupe Islands. Sweden. The kangaroos in Australia.

As Louis was leaving a lovely present on somebody's lawn and I was strapping on my hospital-grade, bulletproof gloves, I kind of started feeling sorry for myself.

Kept walking.

Looked over at Louis at the end of the rope.

He couldn't be happier. So excited about spotting and sniffing the next bush, the next flower, the next patch of green grass.

He wasn't thinking about yesterday, what he had on his plate tomorrow, taxes coming due, nothing. All he was thinking about was that whiff of lovely gardenias that tip-toed across his nose.

In the *moment*.

* * *

I was just killing time, so I figured, why not? I'll drink what he's drinking. See if *that's* fun.

I stuck my face right in a night-blooming jasmine flower. Took a big breath in.

Spectacular.

Did it again for double the pleasure.

Stopped for a moment. Looked right above me at a bouquet of clouds against an endless blue frame.

Picked the most wonderful orange—right off a tree in a front yard.

Happy the owner didn't see me do it and run out with a machete.

* * *

Kept walking. Kept smelling. Kept looking. Kept feeling.

Just a *smorgasbord* of senses.

I blinked, and there I was.

Standing on the *top* of the mountain.

I did it. I *made* it.

I was right on the edge of the bluffs, looking out at the wildest, sparkling, colorful, dazzling vista *imaginable*.

Like it was drawn with the hand of Monet, the Catalina islands were brushed in above the horizon.

I could feel the hint of the ocean tingling on my face—and a touch of perfume from the eucalyptus trees blanketing above.

I looked back over my shoulder at our town framed by the majestic Santa Monica Mountains—shadowing a village of family homes below.

Right in my own *hometown*.

I stood there with Louis.

Taking it in. Taking a breath. Closed my eyes.

And felt the best feeling of them all.

Grateful.

Maybe I'll go traveling again tomorrow with Louis.

Who knows what exotic place we may visit.

SUNDAY FOOTBALL

Next Sunday, when your body has become a part of your couch? And you can't *possibly* get enough sports? And your better half says, "You haven't moved an inch this whole afternoon"?

Tell 'em *this*.

※ ※ ※

For openers, you *are* moving.

That couch you're plopped on is spinning around with everything else on our lovely little planet.

At 1,038 miles per hour. Compare that to the fastest trains in the world at 268 miles per hour.

But don't forget that our earth is zipping around our sun every 365 days. Let's add *that*.

So, how fast are we going around the *sun*?

We're on a speed train at a clip of 66,600 miles per hour.

And that's not even counting how we're playing "crack the whip" at 560,000 miles per hour around a *huge* black hole at the hub of our Milky Way.

Let's not forget our Milky Way galaxy, with 200 billion other neighborhood suns and planets, is flying towards a *humungous* cluster of 100,000 neighboring galaxies at *1.5 million* miles per hour.

And that's before we even *talk* about the toboggan ride we're on in the "expanding universe."

* * *

So next time somebody tells you that you haven't moved an inch, tell 'em they're *way, way* off.

You're going a million miles an hour.

THE WEDDING PROPOSAL

From the "Daddy Years."

My baby girl, Kaitlyn, was born, it feels like *two* minutes ago.

She called my wife and me with the news that she's engaged.

To Jimmy Little, an absolutely fabulous guy from Short Hills, New Jersey, whom Kaitlyn has been dating since their college days together at SMU.

I thought wedding bells were in the air a year ago.

I was traveling in New York (where Jimmy was working at the time), and he invited just *me* to some swanky private club for a drink.

I kept waiting for the big question to come up.

Never did.

I figured he looked across the table at me and suddenly imagined all the gazillion knucklehead Dunnes he'd be related to.

And how they'd probably welcome him in the family by tackling him, pinning him down, and giving him a good old-fashioned wedgie or something.

* * *

Fast-forward to a week ago.

Jimmy Little invited me out to dinner again—this time at a snappy-pants restaurant in Brentwood, California.

When I got there, he was all buttoned up in a suit and tie—and we had the usual early dinner-table chit-chat.

Then he looked at me. Said he had something to talk to me about.

About how much he loved my daughter. About how he couldn't imagine living his life without her.

And he asked me for my blessing for her hand in marriage.

I pulled a sealed envelope out of my pocket that had on the front, "To be opened on a very special day."

As I opened it, I told Jimmy I had three questions for *him*.

I read from the note.

"Do you promise to respect Kaitlyn more than you will respect any other person in your life?"

He looked me deep in my eyes and said, "I will."

"Will you love her and financially support her and your family—through the twists and turns—and ups and downs of life?"

He said, "Yes, I will."

And I asked him, "Are you going to celebrate with my daughter the joy of life?"

He said, "I promise I *will*."

But, the truth is, when I was looking into his eyes, I didn't see him.

I saw *her*.

I saw her cuddled in my wife's arms on the day she was born.

I saw her skating around a rink as a little girl, lost in her music.

I saw her as I hugged her goodbye in her freshman dorm room at college.

And I imagined her on my arm coming down an aisle.

I told Jimmy that my wife and I were so honored and thrilled to give our blessing.

Jimmy and I cried together in each other's arms.

✳ ✳ ✳

A few days later, Jimmy and Kaitlyn were heading to Sicily for the wedding of two of their dearest buddies.

On the first night there, Kaitlyn was getting something out of their shared piece of luggage in their hotel room.

She spotted a ring box hidden in the bottom of the suitcase.

She said her heart stopped—and she literally stepped back from the suitcase, just staring at it.

Do I open it? Do I pretend I didn't see this? She couldn't help herself. After all, she *is* her mother's daughter.

She *opened* the box.

Whoopsie.

It had two of Jimmy's baseball cuff links.

Now, she was absolutely *positive* he wasn't asking her on the trip.

But he *did*.

Here's what happened.

The day after their friend's wedding, Kaitlyn was alone with Jimmy in a stunning Sicilian garden on the hillside of a breathtaking hotel—as the sun was slowly dipping into the Mediterranean waters off in the distance.

Jimmy took both of her hands so that Kaitlyn was looking right at him.

Without words, she knew, in that moment, what was coming.

A sea of tears poured from her face before he even said a word.

Jimmy got down on his knees—and with a warm, aqua-blue sea of promise and adventure over his shoulder, Jimmy offered her a ring—and asked Kaitlyn if she would marry him.

The picture that tore a hole through me is with Kaitlyn's hands on Jimmy's face.

In that moment, I can see her realizing how everything in the rest of her life would change.

And what she was fantastically welcoming in her life—and what she was forever letting go of.

For me, the love for a child is my life's absolutely unexpected surprise.

I never *possibly* imagined the depth and richness and pain and exuberance that you could feel for a child.

And how *her* happiness is my happiness—and when she hurts, I hurt.

Love. Kids. Marriage.

Three powerful, beautiful words.

FIRST JOBS

I was at a pal's house this Saturday.

His senior-in-high-school kid was in the backyard with a handful of buddies, whacking some golf balls into a big net. A *great* kid. I've known him since he was a squirt. Always nice. Full of good looks and charm.

I offered him seventy dollars to take me to the airport the next morning.

He looked up after a nice, lessoned swing with his brand new TaylorMade Stealth 2 Driver with a Fujikura Speeder NX Red shaft and said, "*I'll pass.*"

I asked the other boys.

A handful of head shakes.

* * *

I was riding my bike home thinking about it.

Those boys *never* got the greatest gift I got as a kid.

First jobs.

I had to *work* as a kid. It was part of the deal.

If I wanted that snappy driver, or anything else under the headline of "fun" or "yummy," I was *paying* for it.

Out of my paperboy monies. Grass-cutting monies. Caddying monies. Busboy monies. Shoveling snow monies.

If you're between forty-five and one hundred, I'll bet the ranch you know what I'm talking about.

* * *

Those kids don't know the feeling of getting handed $3.50 on a boiling hot summer day from an old man neighbor behind his aluminum screen door after cutting his lawn.

Of the feeling of just *dripping* in sweat with clips of yellow grass stuck to your face—as generations of mosquitoes have dinner on your arms.

Or folding up and rubber-banding newspapers in the black and bitter of the morning and shoving 'em all in a huge basket on the front of your Schwinn one-speeder. And before the birds sing their tunes, making a sport of winging 'em on front porches— dreaming you're Rick Mount at Purdue.

They never shoveled thick, wet snow with a knucklehead buddy on a driveway in the spank of winter.

Or felt the high of sweat dripping and freezing at the *same* time on your face, or why you need to grip your hands in a fist under sopping-wet gloves so the tips of your frozen fingers don't crack.

Or the seventh-grade rite-of-passage of *barely* lugging two, thirty-five-pound, golf bags on your shoulders—a good fifteen yards behind a foursome of irritated country clubbers who think your first name is "Caddy."

* * *

Seems like yesterday. Eighth grade, dreaming about what all the first-stringers on our basketball team had.

Black Converse All-Star gym shoes.

At the time, thirteen dollars plus tax at Montgomery Ward in town. It took me a couple of weeks of jobs to save up.

When I tied up those shoes for the first time, I was tying up a lot more than those shoes.

Tying up a little dream, a little "action plan" with some bumps along the way.

Felt *good* tying up those shoes.

✳ ✳ ✳

But we all know the pressure the world puts on us to give our kids the *best*.

To be lessoned-up in sports. In academics. In dance. In music. Coaches for *everything*.

Grammar and high schoolers are running a million miles per hour, cramming life in from the second they wake up until they fall asleep.

They don't have *time* to work.

As parents, *we're* the captains of their grade school and high school ship.

Not *them*.

Sometimes, captains have to make tough decisions that annoy the hell out of the crew.

Maybe architect Mies Van der Rohe was right. Maybe sometimes "less is *more*."

More time to breathe. To think. To hustle. To *dream*.

✳ ✳ ✳

Those boys in the backyard? *All* great kids.

They're not passing on seventy dollars.

They're passing on a richness of experiences they can't ever go back and recapture again.

I asked my buddy's kid if he wouldn't mind if I took a swing with his new, snappy driver.

As I stood up to the ball, he said he was probably getting an extra thirty yards off the tee.

I took a swing. Sure felt *good*.

I smiled at the kid and handed him back his driver.

I thought about my first jobs.

Those beautiful, *wondrous* first jobs.

Probably gave me even more than an extra thirty yards off t he tee.

THE MOST PRECIOUS WORD

*D*edicated to Joanie Dunne and all the moms who have passed away—and will never, ever be forgotten.

After raking in a wad of cash from my 750 aunts and uncles for my first communion in second grade, I went with my mom to make a deposit at our local bank.

My mom and I were standing at the teller's window. This middle-aged guy, with a tie knot that was too big, asked my mom what her occupation was.

My mom, Joanie Dunne, said, "I'm just a housewife."

It was the *just* that hit me.

I chimed in, "She's my mother."

He gave me that smirky, condescending look where he was really saying, "You get a gold star for figuring that out."

I didn't have the confidence or permission or biceps to explain what I meant, so I just pulled out my money and put it on the counter.

It's taken a long time to really know what I was trying to tell that man.

It's taken a *lifetime*.

* * *

You get many dozens of years to experience hundreds of treasured moments that *profoundly* move you, that inspire you, that reinvent you.

You have dear, cherished, caring friends who know the *real* you, massage you, and fill you up at every harbor of your journey.

Over a lifetime, you live in a number of places that ground you—creating springboards for your possibilities and relationships.

You become part of many groups, clubs, and activities that are comforting blankets to cook and shape the unique and evolving *you*.

As years go by, you visit so many places around the world, forever a re-reminder of nature's banquet of what wonder and breadth mean.

But you have only one, only *one*, of maybe the most precious and elegant word in the world.

Mother.

The word from where love, and commitment, and giving were born.

THE HUGE KILLER SHARK

All in all, I'd have to say I'm a pretty good athlete.

But if you ever saw me on a paddleboard, you *sure* wouldn't think so.

I love to go out in the early morning in the Santa Monica Bay, spending most of my time trying to stand up on the damn board.

And then, after about five seconds, flopping in the water.

And then I pull myself *back* up on the board. After doing *that* about a dozen times, that's plenty of exercise.

I just spend the rest of the time exhausted, lying on the board, floating around, just thinking about stuff.

Nothing wrong with *that* if you ask me.

The problem with lying out there just thinking about stuff is just lying out there *thinking* about stuff. Because when you start thinking about stuff, you start thinking about stuff you shouldn't be *thinking* about.

Like what's ten feet south of your board looking *up* at you.

And then I start hearing *that* John Williams score.

I look around and realize how far I drifted out in the food chain in the deep blue sea—and how *nobody* can even see me anymore.

I peek over the side, and the water is so calm and clear I can see the bottom. I'm hoping to God not to look down and see some huge-ass uninvited guest at my pool-party-for-one that thinks I look "yummy."

I tuck my fingers up on the paddleboard right about then. Nothing's sticking out.

It's *deathly* quiet.

Even though I'm lying flat on that board, and there's not a wave in the damn ocean, I'm thinking it's tipping.

I'm thinking I'm going to be looking in his mouth like I'm a dentist, only my whole head's going to be in his mouth.

It's now *only* time before I'm a goner. I'm a ticking, frigging clock.

It doesn't matter if I can see him. I *know* he's there. I can *feel* him in that water circling below me, ready to *pop* up on that board. He's toying with me.

* * *

My life flashes before me.

I start thinking about fishing as a kid with my brother and dad in a crappy old rowboat in Dewey Lake, a lake the size of a stamp in the belly button of Michigan.

Catching fish smaller than my fingers.

I remember us shoving a hook in a live worm (that must have felt like a damn hatchet to that worm).

My dad comforted my brother and me with his big ol' Irish grin in his Cubs hat, saying, "Don't worry, it doesn't hurt the worm."

And I remember pulling a dinky, squirmy fish in the boat with a hook jammed through his lip—and my dad smiling. "Don't worry, little buddies, it doesn't hurt the fish."

Yeah, right.

So, as I'm floating around in the Pacific, hearing that *Jaws* theme, waiting for that shark to chow down on one of my thunder-thighs—I'm wondering if he's thinking, "Don't worry, it doesn't hurt the *human*."

THREE-POUND WEIGHTS

I was in this exercise class yesterday, and we were all standing there holding a three-pound dumbbell in each hand.

We had to hold them fully stretched out in front of us.

For the first two minutes, it was a big *nothing*. So what.

Then with each passing fifteen seconds, those little dumbbells started to feel like I was holding bowling balls in my hands.

It didn't help that I was standing next to this at least 115-year-old guy who didn't seem to have any problem holding 'em out there. The more he could see I was about to pass out, the bigger his smirky grin got.

To get my mind off thinking about him and how I was a human Gumby, I started thinking about my days as an altar boy back at St. Francis Xavier parish in Chicago.

* * *

I was really proud of my school record (it may still be the record today) of doing three zillion 6:15 AM masses in a row—from about second grade until I had a bountiful bouquet of zits on my forehead.

My dad would go to a lot of my masses and sit out there in the first pew and give me a wink and a thumbs up when I'd make an impressive genuflect or something.

See, to my dad, being an altar boy was a sporting event. And the goal of all sports is to beat everyone else.

After the match (sorry for the typo, I mean "mass"), he'd drive me home and give me tips for the next morning's game.

* * *

While the priest would walk over to the pulpit to give his homily, the altar boy's job was to light this gold-plated candle.

I think the parish got the candle from Moses himself; it was about two feet tall and weighed about seven thousand pounds.

You'd stand there next to the pulpit holding that thing with your arms stretched out.

Part of the reason you held it all the way out is so the flame wouldn't light your face on fire.

I'd stand like one of those guards at Buckingham Palace in their bearskin hats—and I'd stare up to the choir loft in the back of the church, pretending like I was brain-dead or something.

All I'd be doing was praying that the priest would cut to the chase and wrap it up.

To this day, nothing irks me more than people who just keep repeating themselves like you're too dumb to get the message the *first* time. If they had been an altar boy and held out that candle, they wouldn't have the problem *today*.

After about six minutes, my face would be turning blue, and my eyeballs would start drifting up to the back of my head—and I'd just keep trying to keep focused on how black my soul would be if I dropped the damn thing.

One Sunday, to a full house, on top of all *that* going on, the candle wax started dripping down on my fingers because I could no longer hold the candle perfectly straight.

I had *two* choices.

Either scream some Satanic profanity at the top of my lungs (that probably wouldn't go over very well) or suck it up and let that hot lava drip on my hands while I felt like I was in a coma.

Being the hall-of-fame altar boy that I was, I picked the latter.

Besides that, I knew I'd get some lecture by my dad on the car ride home about what Dick Butkus would have done—while I'd be blowing in the back seat on the holes that went straight through my hands.

* * *

But then the *craziest* thing happened.

One day, when that wax started melting my fingers again, I pulled an *audible*.

I just set the candle down on the ground next to me and held my hands together like I was a cupid or somebody. A clean and crisp move.

The fans *loved* it.

When I got in that car, my dad looked me in the eyes and said, "Jimmy, you're the George Halas of altar boys."

From that day forward, after I'd light that thing, I'd just set that bad boy on the ground and call it a day. Like it was right out of Thomas Aquinas's playbook.

Touchdown.

* * *

I was slapped back to reality, standing in that exercise class holding out those three-pound weights.

The only thing worse than the pulsing pain sizzling up my rubber arms was the thought of looking next to me at that old geezer's puss if he outlasted me—with that bouquet of hairs sprouting out of his ears.

All this yapping about altar boys and three-pound weights is really just so I can ask you a question.

Is there a three-pound weight that you've been carrying—that's getting *heavy*?

Maybe it's a task on your to-do list that you're putting off.

Or maybe it's guilt about something.

Or maybe something you said to somebody that you wish you didn't.

Maybe it's time to do it. Or let the guilt go. Or make a call.

Set the thing *down*.

And blow out that candle.

FIRECRACKERS

As we're all heading into the parties and fireworks leading up to the Fourth of July, you may be feeling a little bit of what I'm feeling.

It's the weekend to celebrate our country that we share.

I don't remember a Fourth of July where I felt this way—or where our country, as a whole, felt this way.

It's a time of reflection for *all* of us.

* * *

I remember how I felt as an eighth grader—it was right around this time of year. A handful of families were gathered around our dinky, flickering, kind-of-color TV.

We collectively watched American astronauts take the first steps on the moon. We watched them plant the American flag.

It's *that* America that I'm still holding on to. Wanting to believe in.

* * *

There sure is a lot of churn underneath the day-to-day of our lives. Immigration, environmental issues, gun violence, economic inequality, abortion rights, healthcare, education—pick one. It's *a lot*.

Add to the mix the most politically divisive years I can ever remember.

We're a car stuck in the mud, and the wheels are just spinning.

The internet, social media, and 24/7 stories on our phones *don't* help.

It seems the more we peel back the onion of who everyone *is* in our country, the more we discover how profoundly differently we think about *so* many things.

It seems we're all hoping young, bright, passionate, provocative, selfless leaders *emerge*.

Following in the heartbeats of Jefferson, Adams, Franklin. In the heartbeats of a young Lincoln and Kennedy.

And may they inspire and lift us all. To once again find a singular dream and intention.

* * *

In sports, when you get in a rut like this, a team takes a "time-out."

Half the trick with time-outs is knowing when to call 'em.

If you do 'em at the right time, they're *just* what you need.

You stop. You gather together in a huddle.

And then you do the most important thing.

You *breathe*. A little longer than you think you need.

After a moment, you look everybody in the huddle in the eyes—and think about what's the best move for the *team*.

You figure out what you need to do to get back on your game.

And, after all that, you think about what maybe *you* can do to help the team get there.

* * *

Maybe *that's* what we need to do.

We all know it sure works *great* for little kids.

When they're all wound up, sometimes the best thing you can give them is a little "time-out."

You have them just sit there—and *slow* down for a minute.

For *just* a second, you get their mind off whatever rabbit they're chasing.

Maybe *that's* what we need. Maybe that's what this Fourth of July should be.

A time-out.

A chance to *breathe*.

Personally—and as a country.

To take a little time to think about where we came from. To take a candid look at where we are right now.

To think about what we need to do to get back on track—to one day get where we want to be.

* * *

This weekend, maybe the trick is to go out of our way to do one act of *unexpected* kindness.

One nice gesture.

Maybe waiting a little bit longer at that stop sign to let somebody cross the street—and giving them a look that lets 'em know they're so worth it.

Maybe giving your UPS or FedEx delivery driver a cold bottle of water and cookie for the ride.

Or maybe on your next walk, flipping your old neighbor's paper a little bit closer to their front door.

Could be, when your partner least expects it, give 'em a little kiss, letting 'em know how lucky you *truly* are.

One act of unexpected kindness.

Add 'em up across the whole town, the whole state, the whole country.

That would be a whole lot of good.

And when you're watching that fireworks show this weekend, pick out *one* firecracker.

One fantastic firecracker.

That's *you*.

Celebrate how *fabulous* that firecracker is.

How it's lighting up the sky.

That's something to cheer about this Fourth of July.

A VISIT FROM THE FUTURE

Here's a "what if."

What if the news, all around the world, reports a woman in New Hampshire successfully time-traveled back in time from 2135?

* * *

From over a *hundred* years in the future.

Facts that come out convince everyone in the world that her story is *100 percent legitimate*.

She *couldn't* be more credible.

The woman tells us she's not willing to tell us *anything* about the future—other than about *one* "discovery" over those one hundred years.

She says the future *definitively* knows, with concrete evidence, the answer to if there *is*—or if there *isn't*—a God and an afterlife.

✳ ✳ ✳

All the head leaders of all the major religions met two days ago with this woman in New Hampshire, along with the world's most respected and pedigreed scientists, cosmologists, and astrophysicists.

They all came out of the day-long meeting *unanimously* agreeing that the evidence is 100 percent conclusive.

They're waiting until tomorrow to tell the world what they all found out. What they all agreed on.

What was black and white.

And if the answer was that there *is* a God, they're going to tell us which religion was definitively right *all* along.

✳ ✳ ✳

The question is…

What will change for you after you hear the results tomorrow?

If it *is* your religion, will you get more engaged in your faith?

If it's a *different* religion than yours, will you join *that* faith instead?

If you are a person of faith, and the answer is that there is no God or afterlife—what would *change* for you?

Would you still gather with those in your place of worship? What would you do differently in your life?

WHERE BEAUTY LIVES

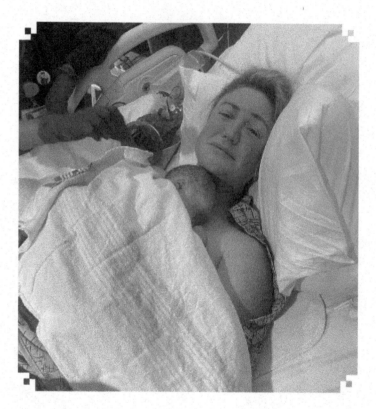

All of our lives are filled with "markers"; moments we celebrate that define our journeys.

Our birthdays. Baptisms or other religious events. Graduations. Weddings. Holidays.

Lots of 'em.

I'm pulled back to my daughter Kaitlyn's eighth-grade graduation in town—where she was giving a speech to her classmates.

She talked about how something that she learned in one of her classes stuck with her. How a lover of music, Pythagoras, said the beauty of music isn't in the "notes." It's in the space *between* the notes.

How, without the "rest," it's not music. It's just a bunch of notes. It's in the *pause*. That's where the heart lives.

* * *

A few days ago, my daughter gave birth to a baby boy. A beautiful, healthy baby boy.

I can't *possibly* express in words the feeling of my wife and me walking into that hospital room and seeing our child, our little girl, with her baby on her chest.

Seeing the way she was looking at her baby.

* * *

Our daughter told us about a moment that happened earlier.

Kaitlyn and her husband, Jimmy, were in their hospital room alone. The contractions were starting to come regularly.

Jimmy was holding Kaitlyn's hand. She looked up at her husband. In the quiet of that moment, they looked into each other's eyes.

They realized they were just about at a door that would forever reimagine their journeys. A door they couldn't wait to open, yet with no way of knowing what they would see and feel.

They broke down in each other's arms.

And without any words, they knew they were ready to go, to forever be there to hold each other.

A moment of promise. Of wonder.

Of what love means.

May you find that moment between the notes—with those you love and need the very most.

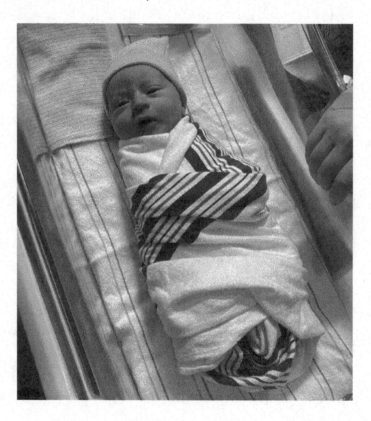

LOUIS, OUR TALKING DOG

I'm kind of embarrassed to say it, but it's true.

Our dog, Louis—he's about a foot long—sleeps on the bed with us. He moves around the whole night, setting up camp in lots of different spots on the bed.

Sometimes he likes to put his head right between the two of us. To kind of be one of *us*. Puts his head on a pillow—and lies on his back with his arms and legs sticking *straight* up.

When he's doing this, you can't tell if he's just happy or dead.

In the middle of the night, the noises that come out of that one-foot thing are *unimaginable*.

From both ends of his body.

. But, from the top end, he makes these moans, murmurs, mumbles, and groans that I could swear he's about an inch away from talking.

He's dreaming about something, and he's *trying* to talk—but he *just* can't seem to get it out.

✳ ✳ ✳

Our morning routine is Catherine's eyes open at about 5:15 AM, and she pops out of bed like the Energizer Bunny.

She gets more accomplished in the next fifteen minutes than I do all day. She pours her first of seventeen cups of coffee, sets her chocolate croissant in the toaster, and takes Louis out for a peppy walk to powder his nose.

In the family room, she sets up croissant camp—and turns on the early morning news, happy as a clam.

Louis comes back in with me, and I lie there thinking about stuff until he steps on me enough that I *have* to get up.

This morning, he was walking on top of me, and I said to Louis, as I always do, "Louis, let's go see Catherine."

He looked at me right in the eyes and said, "Okay."

Stunned, I said, "Louis, did you just *talk*? Can you *talk*?"

He said, "Little bit."

"Louis, what's your name?"

He looked at me like I was an idiot, thinking to himself, *You just* said *my name.*

"Louis."

Excited, I said, "So, give me…the big picture. You *happy*? Do you like us as parents?"

"What are you *talking* about?" he said. "You two are the *greatest*."

He had this raspy, mumbly, kind of Elvis accent kind of thing going on.

"Louis, what's your favorite thing to do?"

"Walks," he said without blinking. "Especially when you take me to the woods. There are like a zillion animals up there. It's a *smorgasbord*. I don't even *know* what I'm smelling."

"It's the Galapagos Islands for dogs."

He was just on the bed chatting away—like it was nothing. *Now* I know how Wilbur Post must have felt in that barn with Mr. Ed.

"So, what's after this, Louis?" I asked. "Do you think there's a doggy heaven?"

"I don't even know what you're *talking* about," he said. "I just figure every day, I'm the *luckiest* dog in the world. Maybe that's why I like cuddling up at night. Because I never know how long I got," he said.

"And I figure, if I go, it would be nice to go kind of cuddled up against both of you."

"That's nice," I said. "Every day, you follow us around everywhere we go. Got any advice for us?"

"Since you're asking, I'd put your phones down. Stop worrying so much. Just enjoy the ride."

"That's a good thought, Louis."

I asked him if there was anything he needed to get off his chest.

He paused for a moment. "Well, I'm getting over it, but I've still got a lot of issues I'm sorting out with you, *you* know, neutering me."

"One day, I go into that room with the guy in the white coat, and I wake up, and my manlies are missing. I can't imagine you'd *do* that to me."

I looked away from him like he does to me when he knows he did something bad.

He was on a roll.

"And did you ever stop to think maybe *I'd* like to try a little of that wine at night? Get a little 'happy' on before *I* hop in the bed?"

I just looked at him. "No, I'm *not* giving you any wine."

Catherine bounced in the room on coffee cup number seven.

"Catherine, watch this. Louis, *say* something."

Louis barked at both of us, hoping for a lovely little morning scratch.

Louis *never* talked again.

* * *

Well, Catherine thinks I'm nuts. I'm sure you do, too.

But Louis and I—*we* know what's going on in there.

After Catherine left to go juice up on another cup, I looked right at Louis.

"Louis, I *know* you can hear me."

He nodded.

"You're not the lucky one, Louis. *We* are. We've got *you* in our lives."

TAKING A PUNCH

I had a handful of summer interns working in one big room in an office.

All of them were in their last couple of years of college; one was smarter than the next.

One of them, just a sweetheart of a girl at the top of her class in law school at USC, ran into my office with tears running down her face. She dramatically said, "I can't work here anymore. Alex just *yelled* at me."

Alex was another one of the interns in the same big room. Going into his senior year at Dartmouth. Kind of large and in charge. Good kid. Kind of on the loud side.

I asked her to take a walk around the block with me.

* * *

On our walk, talking through her tears, she gave me the whole scoop. She told me how Alex was jealous because she was in law school, and he just walked right up to her desk criticizing some work she did—pointing his finger at her.

She thought for sure I was going to tell her how he's canned the *second* we walked back to the office.

Nope.

I suggested to her that she needed to learn how to "take a punch."

She looked at me like I was Satan.

"What?" She looked into my eyes, still with tears.

I told her a story about my dad.

* * *

He'd look us seven kids in the eyes to make sure we were doing *one* thing. *Taking* enough punches—and *throwing* enough punches.

He wasn't talking about physical punches.

Life punches.

I told her how when my brother and I were little squirts, we got a Bobo the Clown for Christmas. We loved it.

It's this life-size blow-up clown that you'd punch—and it bounces right back again with a big, goofy smile on his face.

On Christmas morning, as we were slugging the thing like two idiots, my dad told us Bobo is like *life*.

How you want to take enough punches to toughen you up—*just* enough so that when life hits you with a big one, it doesn't knock you off your feet.

My dad talked about how life sometimes *hurts*. Can hurt a *lot*. But how the joy of it all, the wonder of it all, makes it worth every minute.

I told the intern, "Here's what I'd do. Go back to that office and show him up with your smarts, great ideas, and hard work. Be *you*. Be the fantastic, thrilling, absolutely one-of-a-kind *you*. That's the best way to punch him right back."

She laughed through her tears.

"I'll *do* it," she said. "I'm going to hit him where it hurts."

We both absolutely howled.

I was thinking about Bobo the last time I got a vaccine shot.

Your body gets pricked with *just* enough poison—just to make sure you're on your game in case a gang of God-knows-what comes knocking on your door.

✳ ✳ ✳

Back to that wonderful intern.

She did *just* that. Crushed it that summer.

And she did my favorite thing interns would do. Got a *great* job with a *great* company—and she's on fire, quickly working up the ladder as an attorney.

Every once in a while, she sends me a text.

"Got punched on a law case yesterday. I'm coming back swinging."

"You go, Bobo."

PINGING THE SPOT

Here's a story.

Maybe it's true. Maybe I'm making it up. Not telling.

This guy, PJ, was driving by himself up from my town to Las Vegas for a big meeting.

Cruising down the highway with his favorite tunes blaring and nothing but time.

Left himself a good two-hour cushion so that he could arrive in Vegas, get organized, tuck in his shirt—and be all set to *dazzle*.

Looks up at the sign. Baker, California.

"Home of the World's Largest Thermometer" and "The Gateway to Death Valley."

He was thinking those signs don't exactly scream, "Top Ten Places I'd Like to Live in America."

And wondering who the geniuses were sitting around a conference table thinking of a name for their new town, and how somebody raised their hand and said, "I got an idea. How about Death Valley? *That* sounds fun."

PJ was probably thinking stuff like that.

Two hours to go. Life is good.

Out of nowhere, the front of his car *erupts* in steam, making some skanky-loud clanking noises that make you say, "My day just got *way* worse."

Slows down, thinking what to do.

An exit on Zzyzx Road in Baker is ahead. Pulls off with his car roaring like somebody shoved a bucket of firecrackers under his hood.

He sputters off the exit.

Lucky him. Right off the ramp, Chuck's Gas and Repair Shop.

An old guy with a hitch in his step and who never got the memo about wearing sunscreen—shuffles out of the shop.

PJ turns off the motor and gets out of the car. Shaking Chuck's hand is like shaking hands with a baseball glove.

He begs Chuck to see if he can fix this—and get him on the road in the next couple of hours.

A big ball of visiting tumbleweed ricochets off Chuck's seasonally washed blue jeans as he opens the hood.

The engine is possessed, like one of the bedroom scenes in *The Exorcist*.

Chuck spits out a possum-full of something after he thinks about it.

In a voice an octave lower than a fifties tugboat, Chuck says *if* he can fix it, it'll be $300 in cash.

PJ is *thrilled*—with just the *possibility* of it working out.

PJ asks how long he thinks it will take.

"As long as it takes." Chuck smiles with a shit-eating grin.

PJ's Eddie Haskell idiot smirk makes it clear who is wearing the pants at this rodeo.

Chuck wobbles into the repair shop.

Picks up his bad-boy wrench.

Totters back to the car.

Mumbles to PJ to hop in and try to start it up.

Picture the sight of the Steamboat Geyser at Yellowstone and the sound your microwave makes right before the popcorn is done.

Chuck grabs his wrench like a cowboy spinning a Colt six-shooter out of his holster.

Stares down the snarling engine—that's just waiting to *bite* him.

Waves his wrench over the engine like a priest waves incense over his parishioners.

Chuck couldn't care less that the steam sizzling out is burning his face. He kind of likes it.

Picks a spot on his operating table.

Bending his wrist like a maestro with a baton, Chuck *pings* the head of his wrench—right on his target.

The geyser shrinks and squeals like the wicked witch, shrinking down to nothin'.

Dead quiet.

The car *purrs* like a happy little bunny.

PJ jumps out of the driver's seat.

"How did you *do* that?"

Chuck spins his wrench back in his holster, showcasing his Grand Canyon of missing lower teeth.

"What do I owe you?" PJ said.

Chuck's look says, "What didn't you get the *first* time you asked me?"

"Three hundred dollars in cash."

"Three hundred dollars? It took you a *minute* to ping the spot."

Chuck spits again. This time, a *big* one.

Chuck gets a little too close up, where PJ can taste the beef jerky on his breath.

"Took me a minute to give it a ping."

"Took me a *lifetime* to know where to do it."

* * *

That's the story.

Here's my takeaway.

Chuck figured out what he loved doing and was spectacular at it, put a sign on his door—and went after it.

Got me thinking.

I've got only so many years in the hopper before diapers are my new fashion statement.

If you're like me, maybe it's time we stop puttering down any roads we really don't want to be traveling on.

It's time to get in—and *stay* in the lane where we can *floor* it.

With the wind at our back.

Where a whole lifetime of being *you* tells you *just* where you should be.

See you down the road.

Maybe I love Cheerios because I love watching what happens every time you're down to the last couple dozen of 'em floating around on top of the milk.

They do the *wildest* thing. They all start gravitating toward each other, snuggling up— creating big group circles of 'em.

I still don't know why that happens. But I love it every time.

* * *

Seems to me that towns are a lot like a bowl of Cheerios.

If you're really lucky, you're in a town where there are magical things that somehow, some way, get all the Cheerios in town together.

Maybe those magical things in your town are amazing schools, and churches, and synagogues. Maybe a bounty of clubs and organizations. Maybe programs at your parks pull all the kids and families together. Maybe happy town events.

And one more that I *never* take for granted.

A town paper.

A fabulous, full-of-love town paper.

You're *really* lucky if you have a good one.

I've been blessed to have had a *great* one in the town I grew up in—and also in the town across the country where we raised our kids.

And I'm not talking about some weekly throw-away chock-full of advertisements with a random story thrown in.

I'm talking about a *town paper*.

Brimming with stories and pictures, celebrating the best of our kids, of our families, of our seniors—cheering on those making a difference in the world.

A town paper is the story of *us*.

In these divisive times, when all we hear and read about are folks so angry and behaving so badly, we yearn for a little "treat" that *settles* us.

Comforts us. Blankets us. Informs us. Inspires us.

And every time we read a story about a grammar school kid who's doing something great, or a mom who's taking a gutsy shot at starting a business, or a fantastic bagger in our grocery store—it *bonds* us.

It reminds us we *belong* to something. Something to cheer for.

Our home team.

* * *

I'm sure you know that town papers, all around the country, are an *endangered* species.

And the sad thing about town papers?

Once they go away, they *don't* come back. Just like an endangered species.

You just hear they closed the presses one day. And then, after a few months, it starts to sink in. You notice that something's *missing*.

Lots of reasons they're disappearing.

At the top of the list is that stores and businesses are shifting ad budgets to Facebook, Instagram, and places like that.

So what can we all do about it? Maybe tell some of our pals to get a subscription. Or whisper in the ear of friends who run a store or businesses in town to think about taking out another ad—if they're on the fence.

✳ ✳ ✳

This story made me hungry. I just made myself a lovely bowl of Cheerios.

I'm thinking about how picking a cereal box out of all those great choices in a grocery store aisle—is kind of like picking a town to live in.

Some aren't good for you; some are just plain boring.

And a lot sure look the same.

But, for me, one feels *just* right.

Sure hits the spot.

Nothing like a bowl of Cheerios.

OUR FAMILY TREE

From my "Daddy" years...
My daughter Alexis was doing a "family tree" project in fifth grade.

She had to write about which relatives were the most important to our family—and asked me who I thought that was.

I told her, "I suppose that depends on how far you want to go back."

We talked about Great-Great-Great-Great-Grandpa Patrick Dunne, born in 1777. One night, he sat his wife Amelia and their ten kids down in their Stradbally, Ireland home—and said "We only live *once*."

He said he wanted a better life for his family—and his children's children. He said his gut said to chuck it all and sail to America.

They left everything and everyone they knew, clung on to each other for months in the well of a lumber boat—and arrived on the shores of Canada.

Alexis asked, "So Grandpa Patrick is our oldest relative?"

I said, "Well, not *exactly*."

* * *

I told her about Auley O'Duinn back in AD 1000 and about a whole church full of Dunne Catholic priests (married and unmarried) in the Dark Ages.

She was fading out as I started lovely stories about the Dunnes of the Ui Dunlainge tribe and their happy homes in the Slieve Bloom Mountains—keeping a low profile from those bastard, war-monger, slaughtering Vikings.

By this time, my fun-facts-to-know-and-tell were boring her to death, and I'm sure they are you, too.

* * *

I was walking right behind Alexis as she was trying to get away to the family room. She had her thumbs dancing on her Mario Nintendo tennis game, but I just kept *babbling* anyway.

I jabbered about what a hoot those Neolithic farmers were that came to Ireland about 5,500 years ago—and those early-

Mesolithic Dunnes from Northern Africa in the Stone Age about 8,500 years ago.

Alexis asked me if our African ancestors were black.

"Might have been," I said.

She said, "Does that mean I'm an African American?"

"Sure does," I said.

I told her that idea may come in handy when it's time to apply for college in a few years.

I momentarily had her attention back.

* * *

I said the truth of the matter is we have to give credit where credit is due.

We wouldn't be here if it weren't for the trilobites from the Cambrian explosion about 500 million years ago.

I said *that's* where we got our *creative* genes.

We talked about how the trilobites were probably the most imaginative and eclectic group of living creatures *ever* to enjoy our home here on Earth. So maybe that makes *them* our most important relatives.

But I *couldn't* leave out the tetrapods, the first land animals to crawl out of the sea. Alexis is a good swimmer; I told her maybe she's got some tetrapod genes tucked away in there.

I was trying to talk over Lexi's electric toothbrush as she got ready for bed when I was going on about the first slit fish and how they had the first set of eyes—I'd guess the first Dunnes to see anything. Where would we be without sight?

I recommended the slit fish as a strong contender for "most important relative."

As I tucked her in, we thanked God for slit fish, the trilobites, the tetrapods, the Larnians, the wild-and-crazy Ui Dunlainge tribe, and sweet pea Auley O'Duinn.

I kissed her goodnight on the head and asked her who she thought was the most important relative—and who she was going to focus her report on.

She rolled over to fall asleep...

And mumbled, "Mom."

THE GREATEST BLOCK
IN THE WORLD

One spring morning in 1960, with four kids and three more to come in the hopper, my parents pulled the trigger on writing a gargantuan check for $6,500 to buy a home.

An investment in their future—and their kids' future.

They made the big move out of a small downtown Chicago apartment and bought a very modest starter home in La Grange, Illinois.

It's a spectacular family suburban town with every home about a baseball field away from great schools, churches, and a ton of young kids and families.

My fifth birthday party at our kitchen table with my mom, the grandmas, and Aunt Mimi. Check out the kids' rosaries hanging on the wall.

It wasn't easy, and it was risky. But my mom and dad made it work.

As my dad said with a big Irish smile, "That house? It was the best dough we ever spent that we *never* had."

* * *

Right across the street, that's where the fantastic Piggy O'Brien lived, with a farm of other fabulous O'Brien kids and parents.

Every summer, Piggy scarfed down about ten thousand Spam and liver sausage sandwiches on white bread—and drank at least a rubber swimming pool of cherry Kool-Aid in our kitchen.

Piggy's house now has central air conditioning. That wasn't invented when we were kids, at least on Kensington Avenue.

We had another name for "air conditioning" in the dinky bedroom I shared with my little brother on a wickedly hot, sticky August night.

It was called "cold showers."

Piggy's house just went on sale.

$585,000.

That's at least a *hundred* times more than Mr. and Mrs. Piggy paid.

I'll bet the ranch a great young family, just like ours and just like Piggy's, is going to move into that home on that full-of-love, tree-blanketed street.

Their kids will go to one of the schools and churches right around the corner.

They'll still get candy at Hank's (now My Grandpa's Store), which has turned over owners about as many times as the Sox have lost the pennant.

Their dad will probably walk to the train station—and he'll work downtown in a big, tall building. He'll take the train home dreaming about seeing his flowering, beautiful, promising family.

It's a *lot* of money.

But I'm sure it'll be the best $585,000 they'll *ever* spend that they *never* had.

OUR SANDBOX

My wife and I have a morning routine.

We make our coffee, Catherine toasts up her chocolate croissant, I get to eat something that tastes like wood—and we sit and watch the news.

Then, the adorable anchors tell us today's "breaking news."

Let's see what today's wonderful stories were to kick off the lovely day.

"Global Warming Surpassing Predictions." "Relations between US and China Getting Worse." "Inflation Climbing to

Record Heights." "Homelessness at Record High in America."
"Woman Arrested for Punching Southwest Airlines Employee."

That's fun.

Thanks for the scoop. That just got me all *pumped up* for my day ahead.

This isn't the pep talk we *need* in the morning.

Here's my take.

We're all just trying to make a little bit of a difference in the sandbox we play in every day.

And those "breaking news" items *aren't* in our sandboxes.

So I tried something today, just for kicks. It worked out great. Might want to give it a try.

Turn it off.

Just turn the damn news off.

The coffee suddenly tasted so much better. And Catherine was in such a good mood she gave me a corner nibble of her chocolate croissant.

When your car radio starts in on a "need-to-know" story about some guy in some town in Arkansas who laced meth in three local salad bars?

Turn it off.

When some guy at a cocktail party who thinks he's Moses's cousin or the next Rene Descartes—starts blabbering about what's on his radio dial to the far left or right?

Turn it off.

Take you and your happy drink to the next table.

✳ ✳ ✳

And when I'm catching the evening news tonight, maybe I'll see how good that fast-forward button works.

And the newspaper tomorrow? I'll read it—but I'll just skip all the stories with the subtext of "Life as you know it for you and your children is absolutely *toast*."

And if we did things like *that* all day long, I'll bet life would give us a little *prize*.

A little bit of *time*.

Time for us to do something else instead of listening and reading and watching all that.

Maybe time to take a short morning walk with my wife. Maybe she'll let me hold her hand on the way back.

Maybe time to stop during the day, close the door in my office and the world, and take a little fifteen-minute nap.

Maybe time to call my kids and tell them about some little moment from a long time ago that reminds me how amazing they are.

And maybe time to look in the mirror and remember how absolutely beautiful…

Our sandbox is.

JOB INTERVIEWS

Getting your first job.

I have a special love for this moment in time in life.

I'm convinced somebody drops cards out a plane over the Midwest with my name and phone number saying, "When you get to Hollywood, call this guy."

One of my favorite times of the week is setting aside 10 and 11 in the morning on Sundays to sit for an hour with kids who are "transitioning." Kids either heading into college or who are fresh out of college—trying to navigate their next steps.

I'm forever amazed how we all fork out a ton of money for our kids to go to college, but nobody there seems to help them with what to do north of the day they get their dapper diplomas.

So *that's* why I meet with the kids. We chat about that.

✳ ✳ ✳

For me, I had two interviews that taught me a lot.

Here they are.

"NETWORKING IS GOOD"

My first job interview in California.

I *couldn't* have been greener. It was with a short, at least eighty-year-old music publisher in his one-man-show office the size of a closet.

It was at the very end of a long, basement floor hallway—smack at the intersection of Hollywood and Vine.

He looked and talked *exactly* like May West. Choked down a fresh pack of Camels every fifteen minutes.

He sat behind his old desk in a really big chair so that I would be staring up at him the whole time. Kind of like that scene in *The Blues Brothers* with the nun.

This really dates me, but I gave him a reel-to-reel tape of two songs; it was before cassettes came out. He wound the tape up on his machine.

Puffing away as he started to listen, I politely told him he had the first song playing at "double speed"—sounding like a *Chipmunks* record.

He chucked up half of a Hostess Ding Dongs, growling with his May West voice, "That's how I *like* it. I get through 'em *quicker* that way."

He listened for twenty seconds tops. Yanked the tape out of the machine. Times up.

Pulled a yellow, weathered sheet out from the top drawer in his pre-Neanderthal-vintage desk. The sheet had one sentence on it.

He stood up, letting me see how short he was , how baggy his suit pants were, and that our meeting was over.

With a half-cigarette defying gravity dangling off his lips, he chucked me the sheet and he snarled in his May West voice, "The Ten Golden Rules of Songwriting. Write with somebody famous. If they're not famous, put somebody famous on it *anyways*."

"GIVE 'EM WHAT *THEY* NEED"

I drove out to California after college, not knowing a single person west of La Grange, Illinois.

But here's the *good* news.

I was twenty-two with a couple of college degrees in my back pocket, absolutely nothing to lose, and a forest fire in my gut— itching to rub some sticks together in songwriting and television.

I had no problem climbing over the walls and fences on the studio's lots, knocking on random doors. Had *lots* of rejections.

But call it what you want—rejection gets old after a while.

I hammered plaques of college day accomplishments on the wall of my dinky studio apartment just to remind myself that I wasn't a *complete* dud.

The only things in that tired one-room apartment were a rented grand piano, a two-track Tascam recorder, and a single bed. And a bunch of dreams.

✳ ✳ ✳

Rewind six months earlier, back in La Grange.

During my last summer at home, I taught tennis.

Smack in the hurricane of the Borg/McEnroe/Connors tennis era, all you had to do was own a pair of tennis shorts to be a tennis teacher. Each college summer, I was the head tennis pro at suburban country clubs near our hometown.

Couldn't have *possibly* loved it more. Loved teaching kids, moms and dads—*especially* the kids. Even had my own pro shop. Learned a lot. About business and a whole lot more.

The dad of this great little kid I gave lessons to happened to be an old fraternity brother of a guy named Garry Marshall, a prince of the television world. He was producing *Happy Days* and a bunch of other huge hit shows on the Paramount lot.

The dad told me he'd try to get me an interview, and he did.

Being a good Midwesterner, I dressed in a suit and tie. It was a *boiling* hot summer day.

After waiting in the secretary's office for a good hour, it became really clear that the *last* thing in the world Mr. Marshall wanted to do that day was interview some green knucklehead from some old frat buddy's hometown.

When I finally got the nod to walk in, Mr. Marshall was sticking this framed picture of his new tennis court on the credenza behind his desk. He put it next to a line of other pictures of him with every famous person on the planet.

He talked like he had a lobotomy a couple of days before.

As I walked toward his desk, he mumbled, "I'm never going play. I got too many shows. I got *no* life."

I sat there sweating, like a pig in a blanket, and I knew from the second he sized me up I had *no* prayer for a job.

The whole interview lasted about ninety seconds. A complete disaster.

On my way out of his office, I passed this jackass in his twenties in the secretary's office. He was next in. The only thing I remember about him is that he had a garden full of zits on his face. He mockingly muttered as I passed by, "*Nice* outfit."

I looked at him, and *just* out of spite of that kid, I turned around and headed right back into Mr. Marshall's office.

Mr. Marshall was *already* on the phone.

"Excuse me," I said. "I can give you something *nobody* on the Paramount lot can."

He was probably amused at what some shameless kid had the nerve to come back in and say. He told the guy on the phone he'd call him back in ten seconds.

From behind his desk, Mr. Marshall condescendingly asked me, "And what would *that* be?"

"That thing you said you *didn't* have. A *life*," I said.

"I'll see you at your tennis court this Saturday at ten in the morning. I'll give you a fifty-five-minute tennis lesson, and you'll give me a five-minute writing lesson."

He looked at me. Came around his desk. Stuck out his hand and said, "See you Saturday."

That Saturday, I gave him a tennis lesson, and he gave me a five-minute writing lesson.

The next week, ten minutes of a writing lesson.

A couple of weeks later, it was raining—but he had me come to his house anyway. We sat at his kitchen table for hours—on the art of "story."

That turned into an entry-level "gopher" job on *Happy Days*, years of invaluable one-on-one writing sessions, working with him each hiatus at his office—and one of the greatest gifts of all time, the gift of *confidence*.

A gift that has *no* price tag.

In those early days, Garry afforded me keys to every sound stage, music stage, every television writing room, and every office on the Paramount lot.

It was *my* job to open the doors.

That gopher job sprouted into all kinds of screenwriting, songwriting, and producing opportunities for many, many years.

He was a mentor to me for my whole life—about *way* more than show business.

✳ ✳ ✳

Back to Garry's theme—the art of story.

I know one story he played a big role in.

Mine.

All I did was listen to what *he* needed.

It's funny how with job interviews, marriage, children, friends...

Listening.

Sure is at the heart of it all.

GRADES AND SOUP

I just read an article about how kids in grade schools, high schools, and colleges shouldn't have grades.

There were lots of big words in this way-too-long story about the effects of grades on some kids, and some cultures, and some backgrounds, and some everything.

If your kids have a pulse and a head on top of their necks, they were in at least one of the groups they mentioned.

Here's the bottom-line point they were making.

It's just too stressful for kids to have grades. Grades can hurt their feelings.

What a bunch of you-know-what.

Life is *competitive*.

I think we're getting too soft.

* * *

And humans aren't the only competitive ones out there.

Pick any animal.

Maybe a robin. A frog. A goat. A whale. A grasshopper. An elephant.

When you net it out, we're all kind of about the "big three."

Staying alive. Finding Mr. or Mrs. Right. And having fun on the ride.

All three are competitive. *Wildly* competitive.

If you're a robin, you're snapping your head around morning, noon, and night like you're the girl in *The Exorcist*, making sure you're not anyone's next meal.

You're *also* making sure you're looking mighty dapper to catch the eye of one fine-looking little birdie stopping by the neighborhood.

And on the fun side? Worms are fun. Flying is fun. Vacationing with friends in the South in the winter is fun. And it's fun singing in the morning about what a great day it is to be alive.

* * *

Back to grades. I suppose we can only go by our own experiences.

Here's mine.

I was kind of an odd duck in college. I loved taking too many classes and learning about different stuff.

But, *no* doubt about it, it would have been a *whole* different ballgame if there were no grades. No tests. No accountability.

I *liked* grades. I *liked* looking around the room on test day at the dopes on my left and right and thinking about how I was going to kick their butts as soon as that exam booklet hit the desk.

Growing up, school was competitive. Asking girls out was competitive. Sports *couldn't* have been more competitive.

Grass-cutting jobs, shoveling snow, Boy Scouts, caddying, talent shows, fraternities, you name it—*everything* we all did was competitive.

* * *

At a grade school in town, the most popular game on the playground is Four Square.

So fun.

The grade school sent out a memo saying, "No more Four Square."

It makes kids too *sad* when they lose.

What?

You win some, you lose some. You *figure* it out. You figure out what you're good at—and what you like doing.

Four Square is life in a *nutshell*.

You try to stay in the game, you try to look cool doing it, and you have a blast along the way.

* * *

Here's my takeaway.

It's an amazing time. Like *no* other time before. And it's moving *so* fast for kids today. "Tomorrow" is more of an unknown than *ever* before.

One thing's for sure.

Tomorrow brings more and faster of *everything*. Exponential advancements in quantum computing will *reimagine* science, medicine, the military, manufacturing, education, finance, farming, you name it.

Extraordinary discoveries in just the past few years, with the James Webb Telescope and the particle accelerator in Switzerland leading the charge—are turning fundamental physics and cosmology theories *upside* down.

In the next few years, as AI and quantum computing leapfrogs our capacities in many areas where we have always been the "kings in the forest," it's going to be *humbling*.

It's going to redefine what *intelligence* means. It's going to redefine where we should refocus learning.

Retaining information is going to be trivialized; while virtues of wisdom, integrity, balance and street smarts will be the new holy grail.

And our role, our place, our obligation as guests on our planet, and as guests in our absolutely humungous universe—is going to take center stage.

The more science uncovers clues to the mysteries of the very small and the very big, the more commitment to faiths will be tested and pushed to the limits.

Throw all that in the soup—and divisiveness, and competition, and anxiety, and social pressures on kids—aren't going away.

Pretending we're not competitive is pretending we're not animals. We're trying to survive just like everything else that's here today, and that's been lucky enough to grace this planet for the past four billion years.

✳ ✳ ✳

Speaking of soup, maybe *that's* where we can step in as parents—or as grandparents.

Maybe that's what we can do.

Help 'em be good *cooks*.

Coach 'em on adding in *just* the right amount of each ingredient.

A little bit of smarts. A teaspoon of a moral compass. A couple cups of integrity. Sprinkle in a little *nice*.

And a dash or two of *tough*.

But the *best* thing in the soup? It's what gives it its *delicious* flavor.

A big, big scoop of *love*.

THE QUARTERBACK

At a fantastic USC vs. Notre Dame rivalry this past weekend, I did something pretty *fun*.

I hung out on the field with a pal for part of the game.

Looking up at an absolutely stuffed Coliseum, hearing the roar of 73,000 passionate fans was *something* else.

And some of the plays happened *right* in front of us. I mean, right in front of us.

I felt like they were going to plow us over.

On one play, USC's quarterback was scrambling for his life in the pocket in heavy, heavy traffic.

I was stunned at the sound of these human *beasts* snorting toward him like a stanza of hungry lions charging a helpless gladiator.

He dodged and ducked and swirled—and somehow spotted a receiver thirty yards downfield over an *army* of huge people.

And he had the guts to throw it—delivering a *bullseye* in a receiver's arms. It was *impossible.*

I'll think twice next time I'm sprawled out on my comfy sofa, dipping my thirteenth chicken tender in some snappy sauce—gibbering my *big* opinions to an audience of none about what the team should be doing.

Maybe there's a *reason* the coach isn't calling me up at time-outs to get my incredibly brilliant sage advice on what play they should call next.

* * *

Here's what hit me, standing there on that field.

In the day-to-day of it all, we're not looking at it on a screen. We're *in* it.

We're the quarterback.

You and me, we've got a whole bunch of things charging at us *all* the time. Sometimes from a blind spot—we never even saw coming. Trying to *knock* us down.

* * *

Just a thought.

Tonight, before you go to bed, I hope you look in the mirror and say to yourself, "*Cheers to me.*"

Cheers for ducking all those quarterback sacks along the journey.

And even better, cheers for when you *did* get sacked—you got *up*.

You stood up, a little dazed, shook it off, and called another play.

Cheers to when you just put your arm out and ran full-speed around the corner—creating some of the best, wildest, unexpected plays of your *life*.

What a game. What a game you've played.

And what a *fantastic* highlight reel.

Full of heart. Full of love. Full of joy.

And, even better, you've still got plenty of time on the clock.

THE LIFE OF A MAYFLY

On a walk with my dog Louis today, I called a dear old friend from my hometown whom I hadn't talked to in a while.

I asked him how things were going.

He said, "All things considered, things are wonderful."

I told him I sensed he wasn't telling me something.

After a pause, he admitted that he'd been in a hospital for sixteen days, dealing with a form of blood cancer.

He said he was hoping he'd be released soon—and for the cancer to enter into remission.

I didn't know what to say.

✳ ✳ ✳

Because we were talking over a phone halfway across the country, it probably made it more comfortable for him to tell me what he was really thinking about.

He told me how grateful he was for the bounty of beautiful things in his life.

For his amazing three kids, his wife, the greatest picnic basket of friends, an ever-evolving career he's proud of, and an amazing life in a small town—full of happy and promise.

He talked about how lucky we are to live in a time where medicine is finding answers to so many problems.

I told him how inspiring and courageous his perspective was. And what an amazing gift that must be to his kids and wife.

We ended up talking about the life of one of my favorite animals.

* * *

The life of a mayfly.

It's somewhere between a butterfly and a fly—with an emerald body and wings. And multiple flowing tails to weave and float through the sky.

Here's the *catch*.

A mayfly lives about eight hours.

They don't even have a mouth because they don't need to feed themselves for a second day.

"One and done."

Yet, on a majestic spring morning, as the sun peaks over the river, they hatch from the waters and take to the air.

Their stunning tails propel and whirl them over their river home—with the crisp late-spring air on their backs.

And they *dance.*

They dance in the sky. Along with many, many hundreds of their own. Can you imagine how thrilling and romantic and exciting it must be?

As they pirouette in the air, courtship begins—looking for that "special" one. The guys put on their best moves in the sky. And when they find each other, they make love, gliding in the magic of flight.

After the most *spectacular* day, the new moms dip down to the water's surface to drop their eggs, continuing the same glorious cycle of life their mayfly ancestors began a remarkable 320 million years before.

Under the blanket of the setting sun, the tired yet so-satisfied mayfly spread their exquisite wings flat on the comforting bed of the gently moving water's surface.

She closes her eyes, reminiscing her lovely day, and she's welcomed back into the cycle of life in the rich river's home.

I was telling my pal if we asked one of those mayflies dancing and spinning in the breeze what they were thinking about, I'd bet they'd say life is absolutely *fantastic.*

We both laughed. I could see his smile through that phone.

We had a moment where neither of us talked. It's a silence that is only earned with relationships over time.

And in that silence, my heart broke, picturing him in that bed in that hospital room.

It was beautiful.

And, in that moment, my friend and I danced—as the sweet mayfly does.

Remembering how remarkable and truly beautiful life is.

SUNDAY MORNING IN THE PARK

There's a beautiful flower with a lousy name. I've loved it since I was a kid in the winters of the Midwest.

The crocus flower.

It's a stunning, purple-bulbed flower, brilliantly framed in green leaves.

When snow covers the rich soil, there's one flower that finds its way.

One flower whose will is *so* strong that it pushes, against all odds, until it sticks its head out of the snow.

When it does, it's just *glorious*.

A sea of snow—and there it is, in all its majesty.

This gentle, wildly wondrous gift is there to admire. To give a hope for tomorrow. To remind us what is *deep* in our roots.

It reminds us of what *will* means. What passion means. What *life* means.

* * *

It's an early Sunday morning at our park in town. The moisture from the ocean still beads on the grass. The eastern sun is warming everything in this town sanctuary.

And there they were, to my wonderful surprise.

Five crocus flowers.

Five spirited Boy Scouts from families in town—armed with buckets of soap, water, and scrubbers.

Eighth-grade patrol leader Santiago and his buddies Tyler, Finn, Jake, and Tucker.

They all got up at the crack of dawn on a Sunday to clean the picnic tables and remove graffiti. They picked up pieces of rubbish in the bushes. They scrubbed up the scoreboards on the bocce courts.

They polished the words that define our town at the base of our town flagpole.

They *never* stopped for two straight hours.

✳ ✳ ✳

Here we are, all feeling like our city, our country, and our world are swimming against the current—full of anger and divisiveness.

And here are these boys, getting out of bed on their "day off" to *show up.*

To *show up.*

To *show up* to say we may not be able to clean it *all* up, but we're going to make a little bit of a difference *right* here, right here in our town. In our hometown.

We're going to make a place as nice as it can be so that people in town can sit here for a moment—and remember to look *up.*

To look up at how lucky, how privileged we are.

Those boys didn't care about a bunch of picnic tables.

They were scrubbing because those tables meant a whole lot more.

It was their way of saying thank you.

To their town. To their family. To their school down the street. To what they believe will blossom in their days and lives ahead.

That's why they were scrubbing. I saw it in their eyes.

An old, weathered gardener once told me that you could only know if soil is rich by digging your hands in the ground and holding the earth right in your palms.

Then you know.

* * *

If a crocus could talk, I bet it would tell us this.

I bet it would say what's beautiful *isn't* what's sticking out of the snow.

What's beautiful are the *roots* that go down deep in the soil—drawing from the richness and the wonder of it all. *That's* where its strength lies. That's where its heart lives.

You just *knew* these boys had strong roots.

Roots of loving families. Roots of a blanket of belonging in their town, in their schools, and in their parish or synagogue.

The boys packed up, headed home. I watched them walking away, kicking and shoving and banging into each other like young cubs wrestling to figure it all out.

I looked around our park. It was quiet.

I looked *up.*

I learned a lot from those boys today.

About what *will* means. What *pure* means.

What *wonder* means.

BASEBALL MITTS AND
LITTLE GIRLS' HEADS

*S*omething from my "Daddy Years."

* * *

I've got *lots* of issues. One that's been a bit of a nuisance is that I'm night-blind.

My wife and daughters have always loved the morbid thrill of sitting in a movie theatre and watching me standing in the aisle like a big, stupid goof with arms full of popcorn, candy, and cokes trying to find them.

After a good howl and watching people tell me to "sit down or get out," they'd finally whisper, "Over here."

They wouldn't say "Dad" because they'd *never* admit they were related to me.

Being night-blind, kissing my kids goodnight was always a challenge.

If I didn't trip over something on the way to their beds, the next challenge was wondering where their heads were in their beds. I'd just be staring at a sea of black.

But the *truth* is, I'm really not interested in *kissing* their heads—I just want to *smell* their heads.

✳ ✳ ✳

We all have buddies who are really into smelling their wine before that first sip.

You know the drill; in that smell, they *imagine* the vineyard…

The end of autumn days just before the harvesting of the grapes. They verbalize their wine and its aroma and bouquet. They say words like "buttery," "corky," "flowery," "noble," "piquant," "vigorous," and "velvety."

To each his own.

Even though it doesn't have a thing to do with this story, I've gotta say...

I've got some pals who really know their wines. It's their hobby. They really enjoy and respect the art and craft of wine-making and have a wonderfully discerning palette.

I've got other pals who just know the cost of wine labels.

When I'm sitting at some snappy restaurant looking at them endlessly swishing their wine glass around their snout, I'm smiling at 'em thinking I'd bet the ranch they wouldn't know the difference if it were Welch's grape juice.

Some like to smell wine; I prefer my kids' heads.

Because in *that* moment of smelling their heads, in that *one-second* moment, I remember what they smelled like the day they were born.

Like *nothing* else in the world.

✳ ✳ ✳

Kids' heads. It's kind of like a baseball mitt. Pulls you *back*.

Like being in a sports store. Walking down the aisle of baseball mitts. Can't you just smell that row of *fresh* leather?

One whiff of those mitts, and I'm front row on the third base line at Wrigley Field with my hero Ron Santo.

Ask *any* dad.

Going by mitts in a sports store is like watching home movies.
If men had it their way, that's what cologne should smell like.
Baseball mitts.

I'd *much* rather smell like a new mitt than the sugar-water
designer nonsense my wife buys me that I'm squirting on my
neck every day.

* * *

And tonight, after I stop scribbling this story, I'll send our dog
out the front door to powder his nose, then I'll turn off the lights
downstairs.

And then I'll walk into each of our girls' rooms—who will be
long, long asleep.

And for just a moment, an *extraordinary* moment, they'll
take me out of the day.

To a place where wonder lives. Where beauty lives.

Where *promise* lives.

AT THE MOMENT OF BIRTH

Picture you're any animal.

You're born. You look around. You look down at your body. You look at your mother.

That's the moment. You realize what you *are*.

Wow.

I'm a duck.

Or maybe you realize you're a squirrel. With a hankering for a good nut. Maybe you're a grasshopper. Or an anchovy fish.

Or maybe you're a dung beetle in the Amazon. Look at the pile over there. There's dinner. Sure smells good.

Or maybe, just *maybe*, you realize you're a human.

✳ ✳ ✳

Here's a little game.

Let's say somehow, someway, *before* this moment happens, you get to go back in time—and *pick.*

You get to pick *what* you are, *where* you are, *when* you are— that kind of stuff.

I'm going to start the game with a huge party favor. You *already* get to be a *human.*

Just for the record books, there are 200,000,000-to-1 insects-to-humans in the world.

You just hit the *granddaddy* of lotteries.

Don't forget, as you pick these other answers, you only get to do this thing called "life" *once.*

So, make *sure* you're good with your answers.

Here we go.

1. When.

Pick when you want to be born.

180,000 BC? Might be for you if you're a big fan of nudist colonies.

Or knock 100,000 years off—80,000 BC? Maybe your name is "Uuugh." That would be about the extent of your charming vocabulary.

Middle Ages? Might want to push the pause button if you're a woman.

How about 1850? Simpler times, maybe you'll meet Charles Dickens. But make sure you're okay with no electricity. Or bicycles. Don't even think about that phone or car. Life expectancy clocks in at thirty-seven years.

Or maybe the year you were born?
Write down the year you'd pick.

---

2. What country.

China? Mexico? Pakistan? Ethiopia? Uruguay? The United States? Qatar? North Korea?
Pick *anywhere* you want to grow up, raise a family, have a career.

---

3. Pick any family.

Pick *any* parents in the world you want. As a bonus, today only, let's throw in that you can even pick some brothers and sisters.

---

4. Pick the town you'll be born in.

Any town in that country that you choose.

While you're at it, pick the house you'd like to grow up in. That'll determine who all your friends are—and probably how one thing will lead to the next for the rest of your whole life.

5. A bonus pick.

You can even pick the person you get to marry. Anybody in the whole wide world. That's a *big* one.

✳ ✳ ✳

That's the quiz.

Now, if you wouldn't mind, go find a big mirror in your home.

See who's looking back at you.

If you're really, really, *really* lucky, the life you picked was to be...

You.

More than one hundred billion people have been guests on this amazing planet, and of *all* the people, *all* the families, in *all* the places, in *all* the times—you get your dream life.

Being the one-of-a-kind, absolutely spectacular, full of love...

You.

TEACHERS

I oversee the garden in our park in town. Six months ago, the plants weren't green enough. Weren't full enough.

We brought in a new landscaper. An artist's soul. We walked through the garden. He put his weathered hands *deep* in the dirt.

He said our garden didn't need new plants. We needed better *soil*. He said it's *all* about the soil. He said with great soil, plants can blossom beyond their *wildest* dreams.

* * *

This morning I walked through that same garden. It's now beaming with green, lush, full-of-life plants.

I was pulled back in time to the soil in a different garden.

Grade school days.

When my parents went to year-end parent-teacher conferences at St. Francis Xavier, my brother and I preemptively layered on a thick stack of underwear under our pajamas, covering our rumps—preparing for the bad news that was sure to walk in that door.

My third-grade class? Three classrooms. Forty-six kids in each one. They hadn't invented air-conditioners yet.

My parents sat me down at home.

They told me my teacher, Mrs. Husfield, said she moved my seat across the room so I'd stop staring out the window all day long.

She told my parents she didn't know what to do with me.

She said she was on the fence about either recommending holding me back a year—or having me skip a grade.

A few days later in class, in a quiet moment, Mrs. Husfield came up behind me at my desk.

She whispered in my ear, "You keep looking out that window. I have a feeling you're going to find what you're looking for."

Never forgot that.

* * *

In eighth grade, I met Sister Virginia. A spunky, too-young nun, full of dreams and love. Fiery red hair peeked out of her nun garb that tried so hard to cover up who she was.

She gave me maybe the *greatest* gift you can give someone.

She *believed* in me.

Virginia has been a pen pal for life. Left the convent and nunhood and lived happily-ever-after with her partner, reimagining ways to make a profound difference in children's lives.

* * *

My creative writing teacher in high school, John Wheeler, gave me an F on my first paper. He told me *safe* gets me an F in his class.

Told me to write something that looked like a mirror. Opened my eyes to the essence of creativity.

* * *

Down the river at college at the University of Kentucky. A sophomore biology professor stood in front of our class and said the reason he was a teacher was so he could tell this *one* story a year.

Showed us a picture of a scab.

Told us how it worked. How you cut your arm and an *army* from your body somehow, some way, all gather on that very spot to do its work.

First, the army builds a tent over the scab. Then they get to work. They call in the "medics" squad in your body. They see what's wrong, talk about it, fix it, and stitch up the cut. No medicines necessary.

After they're all done, they bring back the crew to tear down the tent over the scab.

Down comes the tent, and you're good as new.

He said, "*There*, right *there. There's* the wonder of life. *There's* a Picasso."

"*Right* on your arm."

He was a doorway to a lifetime gift of searching for that wonder in the boundless treasure chest of science.

* * *

And the richest bed of soil? Right in my own childhood home, selflessly tilled by my mom and dad.

The lover and the boxer.

A dad who would look us seven kids in the eyes as we walked out the back door—and say like he was Russell Crowe in *Gladiator*, "Be a Dunne."

And a mom who would walk me to my bike, kiss me on the head, and tell me to "*be kind.*"

My mom always said that the greatest two gifts a parent can give their child are love and—the *greatest* of them all—*respect.*

I'm sure you'd agree teachers come in all shapes and sizes. Brothers, sisters, friends, coaches, co-workers, authors, bosses, gardeners.

* * *

Teachers.

Great ones steer our lives.

Just enough that we barely know it, but just enough to make *all* the difference.

Most teachers teach nouns. You know, like the names on the doors and books.

The main thing they make you do is memorize stuff. The better you memorize it, the better grades you get.

The great teachers teach you *verbs.*

To dream. To find the wonder. To open your eyes–and reach.

They take a book and make it about you. Your story.

And the *rare*, really great ones make you discover someone in you–who you didn't even know you were.

* * *

If you wouldn't mind, I hope you take a moment right now.

Thirty seconds.

I'll start my watch.

Try to look back at those teachers—in your remarkable journey.

Visit the ports in the harbors your ship has traveled to because of the confidence and gifts–and maps they left with you.

LENT

There's a great old tradition in the Catholic church.
Lent.

It's where you give up something for the weeks before Easter.

Lots of other religions have similar practices.

Maybe it's candy, or cocktails, or desserts, or cigarettes, or soda, or watching some idiot, mind-rotting TV series, or french fries or bread.

Could be anything.

You end up feeling better. You feel like you stuck to something and *did* it. And, sometimes, you give up something that you might end up giving up long after Lent is over.

✳ ✳ ✳

One of my favorite moronic movies is *Kicking and Screaming* with Will Ferrell—it's where he's an obnoxious coach of a little girls' soccer team. He has an epiphany and gets his team of little girls around him in a huddle at their big game.

His words of advice are, "Whatever I told you before—do the *opposite*."

Maybe *that's* the trick. Instead of taking something away from our lives—we *add* something.

Maybe it's *adding* something that makes our world a better place.

Maybe it's writing a short, handwritten note that you stick in the mailbox to somebody who doesn't expect it.

Maybe it's making a point to knock on the door of that older woman who you know spends too much time all alone.

Maybe it's on your early morning walk with your dog and picking up everybody's morning paper and setting it by their door.

Maybe it's promising yourself that in every restaurant you visit, you'll stick your head in the kitchen, look in the eyes of the cooks, and let 'em know how much you appreciate what they made for you.

Maybe it's calling somebody in your family—and letting 'em know about all the little things they've done over the years that you are so grateful for.

Maybe it's making a point to really look your spouse in the eyes when she's talking and telling her, with *just* your look, how beautiful she truly is.

We're all hurting every day watching and reading about the families in Ukraine. We're all anxious about where this all leads. We're all sad to be reminded of the barbaric, unconscionable damage one person's actions can have on the world.

At the same time, images of the baby strollers that Polish women left at their local train stations for incoming Ukrainian moms remind us all of what *humanity* means.

And reminds us how connected we all really are.

We're all wrestling with what we can do to help. We're all wrestling with feeling so hopeless—trying to figure out how we can touch the Ukrainians in *some* way.

Maybe doing a small act of good right in our towns, right in our own lives, will, for a moment, temper our fears and anxiousness.

And I hope when that Ukrainian mom walks off that train and sees that empty baby stroller greeting her—she *knows*.

I hope she knows that behind that beautiful Polish woman who dropped it off—is a whole world of beautiful people.

Just like *you*.

THE JEWELRY BOX

*F*rom my *"Daddy Years."*

My wife, Catherine, *loves* her jewelry.

Not for its financial value but for its emotional value. Every piece of her jewelry *reminds* her of people and moments in her life.

My thirteen-year-old daughter had filled up a shoe box on the shelf in her room with favorite cards, letters, and small jewelry pieces.

I gave her a jewelry box for her birthday and left this poem/letter inside.

Dearest Kaitlyn,

This gift may be a jewelry box
But it's a home in many ways
A place to keep your memories
That lasts all of your days

And may this box grow one day
To look a lot like you
A mirror of your life
And the journey you've been through

For you're the brightest diamond
The most exquisite pearl
You're a gem that shines so bright
You can light the world
You're the jewel...
So beautiful to me

And may the richness in this box
Be not the gems and rings
But in a joy and happiness
That memories can bring

And when you open up the box
You'll find a special place
It's a mirror that holds an image
Of God's most precious face

And if your life is so blessed
To have a little girl one day
I hope you pass this box to her

And maybe you will say…
You're the brightest diamond
The most exquisite pearl
You're a gem that shines so bright
You can light the world

You're the jewel…
So beautiful to me

LOOKING UP AT THE SKY

If you're blessed with kids, when you go in their rooms tonight to kiss them goodnight, smell the top of their heads.

And in that quiet moment, may it take you back to when they were born.

Remember how you felt, how your spouse felt. How your baby must have felt in both your arms.

And tomorrow, when your partner in life *least* expects it, kiss 'em on the lips like you haven't kissed 'em in a long time—and hope they kiss you back.

And call up your best buddies and take them out for dinner. Make toasts all night.

Everyone's toast should be about how *great* everyone else is. And if anybody left out anything about how spectacular *you* are, make an *extra* toast to yourself.

* * *

And tonight, after everyone's asleep, go out to your backyard.

Just *stand* there. Look around. Look up in the sky.

And think about how it's not your backyard. How you're just standing on this planet. This planet busting with life. Busting with energy. How gravity is the only thing that's keeping you from floating away.

How eighty-six billion neurons on the top of your head are firing two quadrillion synaptic events every *second*. How only two percent of the atoms that make up you were even *in* you a year ago.

And, in the quiet, listen to the music the wind plays. And to the soothing clock and rhythm of the crickets.

And then look *up*.

To the wonder. To everything you'll *never* know.

And may you imagine the stars are other roads you could have taken.

Other careers. Other places you could have lived. Other relationships. Other kids you could have had.

And, with your feet on the ground, spread your arms in the air and feel it all. The ground you're so firmly on. Your heart perfectly beating in your body. Feel the light breeze hitting your face.

And feel how extraordinary it is to be *you*.

To have what you have. To dream of what you still have time to be.

And close your eyes.

And, in that moment, may you feel a bit closer to knowing who you are, where you are—and where you're going.

ACKNOWLEDGMENTS

This is really about gratitude.

As I talked about in a few of the stories, I hit the jackpot as a kid.

Two loving parents, six spectacular brothers and sisters that I can't love more, and raised in the best town a kid could be lucky enough to grow up in.

I had so many selfless teachers along the way from grade school through college days.

Garry Marshall gave a 22-year-old kid a lifelong mentorship in the art of story—and an ocean-full of confidence.

Top of the list of lifelong teachers I never met would be Carl Sagan, Will Durant, John Prine, Mr. Rogers, Joseph Campbell, Will Rogers, Carlo Rovelli, and Finley Peter Dunne.

Cheers to my brother Marty for endlessly putting up with phone calls that start with "what if." I'm so grateful for my talented buddy John Arends, whose reverence for story has been such a compass. Thanks to friends Tegan West and Mark Tabit—for their generosity and sage advice.

I've been so blessed with the bounty of extraordinary friends. And to my dearest, best pals; I am so grateful. Rick Caruso has been in the fun and the trenches of every chapter of my life for forty-five years. Ted McGinley slept under my piano in my first home, and he's had to listen to every sing and story I've ever written ever since then.

My editors, Caitlin Burdette and Debra Englander at Post Hill Press, have been such wonderful collaborators on this book journey—along with my spectacular agent, Austin Miller at Dupree Miller & Associates. Golda Ouano, thank you so much for your artistic, creative hand in the interior design of the pages.

And the spectacular Jan Miller. I adore you. You are to literary agents what Manolo Blahnik is to shoes.

Lastly, to the heartbeat of my life, Catherine Bailly Dunne. The day I met you I got crowned "the luckiest guy in the world." Our girls Kaitlyn and Alexis, son-in-law Jimmy Little, and grandson Whit have evolved my life beyond anything I ever, ever could have imagined.

ABOUT THE AUTHOR

Jimmy Dunne is *just* what we need in these challenging, divisive times. One of seven kids from a suburban Chicago midwestern family, Jimmy Dunne headed to California to find success—and that he sure did.

A modern-day Renaissance man, Jimmy is a songwriter with dozens of gold and platinum records—with songs on twenty-eight million records worldwide. His themes, scores, and songs have graced over a thousand television episodes, several hit movies, university alma maters, and songs in the Olympic Games. He's had screenwriting and producing credits on hit television series, written an award-winning children's book, recorded numerous solo records as a piano artist, and founded successful music and branding companies.

But if you ask Jimmy, more important than anything, he's a dad to two daughters, a new grandpa, and a husband to his award-winning, interior designer wife and living in Pacific Palisades, California.

Contact Jimmy Dunne at:
jimmydunne.substack.com
instagram.com/jimmydunne7
facebook.com/jimmydunnemusic
jimmydunne.com